Adopt the Baby You Want

MICHAEL R. SULLIVAN
with
SUSAN SHULTZ

SIMON AND SCHUSTER
New York London Toronto Sydney Tokyo Singapore

Simon and Schuster
Simon & Schuster Building
Rockefeller Center
1230 Avenue of the Americas
New York, New York 10020

Designed by Irving Perkins Associates
Manufactured in the United States of America

3 5 7 9 10 8 6 4 2

Library of Congress Cataloging in Publication Data

Sullivan, Michael R., date.
Adopt the baby you want / Michael R. Sullivan with Susan Shultz.
p. cm.
1. Adoption—United States—Handbooks, manuals, etc.
I. Shultz, Susan. II. Title.
HV875.55.S85 1990
362.7'34'0973—dc20 90-33619
CIP

ISBN 0-671-65761-5

Special thanks to all of those people without whose help this book could not have been written: Allen and Mary Williams; Beverly Quidort; Beth Kozan; Julie Owen; Shirley Goldsmith; Natalie Grant; Polly Weber; Larry Gagnon; David Leavitt; Elizabeth Cole; Lois Truffa; Edna Gladney Adoption Agency; Spence Chapin Adoption Agency; Karen Tinkham; Ellen Curtis; and to the hundreds of people who so graciously responded to our questionnaires.

Special commendation goes to my friend James R. Medlock III, cofounder of our adoption programs and business partner, for taking time from his busy schedule to organize consultants, staff, and the research vital to making this book possible.

Contents

Introduction

Adoption.

For many people, it is a process that provides the only real hope of ever having a child to love and care for; the only real hope of fulfilling the dreams of parenthood. But finding that perfect child is not always easy. The path to adoption can be strewn with frustrating obstacles, both legal and personal.

In the 1970s, early in my legal career, my representation of adoptive couples helped me to understand and facilitate many independent adoptions.

Because of the changes in and increasing complexity of adoption practices, I saw a need to offer better services to birth parents and adoptive parents alike. Therefore, my partner, James R. Medlock, and I cofounded three full-service adoption agencies in the 1980s. They are:

Southwest Adoption Center, Inc.
2999 North 44th Street, #450

Phoenix, Arizona 85018
(602) 234-2229

Adoptions of New England, Inc.
190 High Street, Fifth Floor
Boston, Massachusetts 02110
(617) 739-2229
(Will have a new address in the summer of 1990)

Adoption Center of Washington, Inc.
2001 Sixth Avenue, #2300 Westin Building
Seattle, Washington 98121
(206) 624-2229

During the fifteen years I have been involved in adoption work, I have seen adoption practices undergo revolutionary changes because of higher infertility rates for those who wish to be parents and increased abortion rates, limiting the number of newborn infants available for adoption. As a result of these changes, I have been asked over and over again, "Please help us understand the adoption process."

Because of the misconceptions and misinformation about adoption, I decided to write this book to help all participants better understand their options. This book offers a step-by-step guide to assist prospective adoptive parents in choosing the best way to expand a family by means of adoption. It presents a variety of options, including foreign and special-needs adoptions. Prospective Caucasian parents wanting children of other races, for example, will encounter no shortage of healthy, adoptable children.

I must offer a word of caution to you before you read this book. Adoption laws vary from state to state. New laws are being passed every year. It is up to you to consult with a licensed attorney, adoption agency, or adoption professional regarding the laws in your state.

—MICHAEL R. SULLIVAN

CHAPTER ONE

First Steps in Considering Adoption

Our goal in this chapter is to help you decide whether adoption is for you. After weighing the pros and cons, many people will choose to adopt—and many won't. In most ways, an adopting family is no different from any family. But in some very important ways, an adopting family is different, and that difference must be confronted.

Before you commit to adoption, consider the following questions.

WHY DO YOU WANT TO ADOPT?

• Do you want to adopt because you want the special experience of loving and being loved by a child? Then you have a valid reason.

• Do you have, say, three boys and you want a girl? If you want the balance and perspective a girl would bring to your family, that is one thing. If you're looking for a toy, a doll to dress up, that's another.

• Do you feel that you will be doing the child a favor? Will you expect gratitude in return? Examine your motives carefully. Are you adopting for your own sake, or for the child's?

• Do you already care for a child in some capacity (as a teacher, foster parent, or volunteer) and think, "Tommy would be better off with me than where he is now."

If this is your attitude, be careful. You may only feel sorry for the child and may not be prepared for a lifelong commitment. On the other hand, you may be an ideal parent because you know and care about children.

• Have you always wanted a baby and found you can't have one? Is this your attitude: "I've endured years of testing and trying and self-doubt and misery, spent thousands of dollars, and now I'm going to have a child, no matter what the cost!"

If you have ever felt this way, you should consider adoption *only* after you have come to terms with your infertility. Only when you don't resent your spouse for his or her infertility or feel guilty about your own can you love and accept an adopted child.

• Have you lost a child? As with infertility, be careful. Don't rush into things. Embrace adoption only when and if you're ready.

• Do you want a baby so you will have someone to inherit your life's fortune? Are you looking for someone to carry on your family name? Those are not good enough reasons to adopt.

• Do you want a baby because it will help your relationship? Adoptions undertaken to save a doomed marriage can only lead to disaster. The pressures and disruptions of life with an adopted child aggravate existing problems—they don't solve them.

• Do you want a baby to make someone else happy? Are you frustrated because of the expectations of your parents, brothers and sisters, your neighbors, and your friends who somehow see a marriage without children as incomplete and flawed? Do you think you may as well try adopting to see whether they are right?

• Are you seeking instant love? Is your spouse too busy to pay attention to you? Are you bored or lonely? Would you like the attention, the baby showers, the playthings, fixing up a nursery, and buying baby clothes? You are expecting too much. A child may not be able to live up to your expectations, and instead, may become cause for resentment.

• Do you want a baby as an accessory? Remember: Babies are up all night, they can be sick, and they are separate human beings.

• *Do* both *you and your spouse really want a child?* Have

you always wanted a son to take camping, play ball with, carry on your business, be a pal, but your wife is less sure? Could she be thinking, "If that's what he really wants, how can I deny it to him?" Is your husband ambivalent about having a family, but has he decided to go along with the idea of adoption because he knows that you love children and that you would be a terrific mother? Unless you have a mutual, shared commitment, you shouldn't consider adoption.

WILL YOU BE A GOOD PARENT?

• *What type of child do you want?* If you expect your child to have a perfect birth parent family history along with impeccable behavior as he grows up, then your attitudes toward adoption are unrealistic. Chances are good that you will be overly demanding as a parent.

• *Do you like children?* Not everyone does. Some people simply aren't suited to parenting. Have you spent time around children? How are you with your nieces and nephews? If you work or volunteer in a setting with children, you're more likely to make the transition into parenthood successfully. If you haven't had much exposure to little children, seek some out.

• *Do you have space in your life for a child?* Maybe you've been married several years, and you and your spouse have jobs you find challenging and rewarding. You go out frequently; you look foward to at least two ski trips a year, and a summer vacation as well. Do you have a rigid schedule and resent interruptions? Look around your home. Do you pride yourself on your white carpet and couch, your crystal collection? Is there really room in your lives for a child? Are you sure the sacrifices are worth it?

• *Can you love and bond with a child not physically related to you?* This is one of the most critical considerations. You can't pass on your genes to this child; he or she will not be a combination of the two of you. Does this matter enough to make you rethink adopting? Can you love someone who doesn't look like you, someone whose personality is different? Or will you welcome an individual, a separate person into your life? Will you cherish the differences that make the child unique?

• *Can* you *accept adoption?* Occasionally, we hear of a child whose parents have never been able to tell him he's adopted. It's a sure sign the parents are not comfortable with the issue themselves.

"It will hurt him to know," they say. You know, of course, who is *really* hurting.

• *Do you worry a lot about what other people think of you?* You'll be surprised at how many people will make insensitive remarks about adoption: "Poor little child nobody wanted." "Who are his real parents?"

You'll be confronted by inquisitions, advice, insulting remarks, and general ignorance. If you can't deal with these things in a way to ensure your child's self-confidence, reconsider.

• *Can you afford a child?* Will you be able to give him

or her the things you want your child to have? Will you resent driving an older car, skipping a summer vacation, or cutting back on your shopping sprees? Are you willing to budget for another human being with escalating needs?

• *Do you have a solid support system?* If your immediate family is fervently opposed to adoption, you may not be able to succeed. Think hard. Consider the kind of support you will find among your friends and your peers. Have there been other adoptions in your family or social circle? How did they work out?

• *Do you have enough energy to make it work?* You may be older than other parents of a new baby. This is a very real concern for many prospective parents. Can you deal with being tired much of the time?

• *Do you have the patience to deal with a child when you are used to the adult world?* Would it drive you crazy to hear the same question again and again, or to be asked to tell the same story fifteen times?

You have confronted two major issues in this chapter: why you want to adopt and how your attitudes will affect your decision to adopt. *Now it's time to consider whether you are* eligible *to adopt.*

It's not just a matter of dialing your local adoption agency and signing up for a baby. However, in almost every situation, if you are determined, you *can* adopt. You may have to work harder at it than you expected. You may have to be extremely creative, persistent and patient. You also may have to compromise. But once you have decided, know that *you can succeed.*

Most agencies have strict criteria, which we'll detail in the next chapter. But before you go any further in the adoption process, you need to reflect upon your overall profile as a prospective parent. Are you a realistic candidate? Can you adopt the child of your dreams?

If you're an attractive, successful, happily married professional in your late twenties, terrific. If, however, you're in your late forties and divorced and seeking to adopt an infant, you may face tough choices and compromises.

Adoption practices are changing dramatically and criteria vary from state to state. In general, the criteria are becoming more flexible, more realistic. For example, even ten years ago, if you were divorced or single, or if you were a working mother, most agencies would have automatically eliminated you from consideration. But today, there are valid options both within and beyond traditional agencies. However, demand overwhelms supply, and requirements can be stiff.

Many people don't understand why they must undergo such scrutiny. The answer is simple: because there are choices involved. There is a mother out there agonizing whether to give up her baby. She is measuring what she can give her baby against what an adoptive parent can provide. And there are others helping her make that choice.

This is not a test of perfection. No one expects that

of you. Birth parents, however, have a right to expect that you can give their baby a better life.

Remember, you're not out to beat the system. You should participate in the right way: with honesty and thoughtfulness.

ARE YOU ELIGIBLE TO ADOPT A CHILD?

So, what kind of a candidate for adoption are you? Although single parents do adopt, the overwhelming majority of adoptions are with two-parent families. The issues most agencies and counselors will want to consider concern the two-parent family.

- Do you have enough money to support another person in your household?
- Will you be able to spend time with your child? If required by the agency, can one parent plan to be at home the first year or two? If this is not mandatory, an agency will certainly want to make sure you can take time off when necessary.
- Are you married? It's against the law to live together without being married in some states. If you are a couple, you may need to be married, typically for several years, to adopt. But such criteria are not always rigid. At Southwest Adoptions, Inc., a couple who had lived together for five years married just so they could adopt, and were matched with birth parents who approved the adoption.

- Do you have a good marriage? Does your marriage appear stable? Even if your marriage works for you and your spouse, would an independent social worker be likely to consider the marriage unusual or unstable?
- Have you lined up baby-sitters and/or day-care options?
- Do you agree on how to discipline your child?
- Have you agreed on a division of responsibilities in caring for your child?
- Do you and your spouse agree about the religious upbringing of your child?
- If you already have a child or children, how will a new child fit in?
- How do you cope with life? What problems have you encountered, and how have you dealt with them? The ideal couple used to be one that had sailed through life unchallenged. Now, the general belief is that this couple, when confronted with change or crisis, won't have the experience to deal with it.

Red Flags: Probable Disqualifications

The following may disqualify you from adopting a child. Keep in mind, though, that in many situations, there are exceptions and alternatives.

- *You don't have enough money.* Although you are not

expected to be wealthy, you are expected to be able to provide for the needs of a baby. You should have some money in the bank for emergencies. One or both of you should have a full-time job. If you are on welfare, you are a poor risk. Ditto if you are unemployed or work only two or three days a week, without other sources of income, or if you are bankrupt, irrevocably in debt, or encumbered by a history of repeated bankruptcy.

• *You are a drug addict or an alcoholic.* If you're a *former* addict or *recovering* alcoholic, that's different. But if your problem is a current one, you need to explain what you are doing to deal with it.

• *You have a criminal record.* A minor offense won't disqualify you, if you are straightforward about it.

• *You have a terminal illness.* Most adoption professionals would consider a serious or terminal illness to be highly disruptive to the well-being of a child. Therefore, if your medical condition makes it probable that you could not parent a child through his teens, you would be a bad risk.

• *You have a serious mental disorder.* If, however, your mental disorder can be controlled with medication and involves little or no risk to you or the child, then you may still be a candidate to adopt.

• *Your marriage is on the rocks.* If you're on the verge of divorce, or if you don't get along with your spouse, you're a bad risk. An adoption counselor won't want to chance placing a baby in a broken home or in a home liable to break up.

During a recent interview, a prospective adoptive husband volunteered, "My wife will kill me for telling you this. But things are really bad with us, and she told me if I didn't go through with this, she would divorce me."

• *You're a divorced parent, and you're not taking responsibility for your children's needs.* Say, for example, you have remarried and are trying to adopt, but you owe child-support payments to your former spouse.

• *You lead a disorganized, messy life.* Your home is filthy. You are irresponsible in your work and social commitments, or have a wild lifestyle.

Other Problems

These are less likely to disqualify you but are certainly grounds for hesitation on the part of the counselors who will approve or disapprove your application to adopt.

- *You're too old.* People forty and older could be disqualified by age alone at some agencies. If, as a couple, your ages differ by twenty years or so, you're likely to be disqualified.
- *You've had multiple job changes and show little financial security.*
- *You're single, divorced, or widowed.* More and more singles are adopting today, but you are still considered less than ideal.

- *You've been hospitalized a great deal.* In other words, you may be too sick to care for a baby.
- *You have a non-traditional lifestyle.* You will be suspect if you live in a commune, are involved with a cult, or are active in an extremist organization.
- *You've been divorced several times.* In this case, your current relationship probably will be closely examined.
- *You are overtly bitter and resentful about infertility.* This does not necessarily mean that you should not begin to explore the possibility of adoption, but it does mean you should work through these feelings.

The ultimate measure is what's best for the baby. And the one with the yardstick is likely to be a counselor who has facilitated many adoptions. His or her goal is to place children, not to block adoptions. But your success in adopting hinges on the people who will judge you. Your success revolves around a somewhat subjective and judgmental system.

If you're essentially qualified, you still may find you're not being offered the kind of child you want. Beware of scams. People may try to feed on your vulnerability and you may be pushed into a situation for which you are unprepared.

Say you've been on an agency waiting list for three or four years. The clock is ticking. You know you're at the upper borderline age. Once again, you phone the agency. "Sorry," they reply, "we don't seem to have any available *infants.* We do have an older child, or perhaps you'd be willing to adopt a child with a physical or mental handicap."

You're ready to do almost anything, and the waiting is unbearable. You believe that saying no means you will never have a family, period. This is precisely the time to put on the brakes. Reassess your options.

WHAT ARE THE ALTERNATIVES TO ADOPTING A HEALTHY AMERICAN NEWBORN?

If you don't qualify for a healthy newborn child through traditional adoption agencies, then what?

• You can give up the idea of adoption altogether. Certainly, this is a time to re-evaluate your desires. At this stage, some people decide not to adopt, and they find fulfillment in other ways.

• You can become foster parents. Be careful. This is not a simple trade-off. Foster parenting requires enormous sacrifice and giving, tempered by the constant knowledge that the relationship is a temporary one. Or you might find fulfillment through volunteering in a hands-on, highly interactive activity with children. You might consider volunteering for a children's organization or working with terminally ill children at a hospital.

• Or, if you're convinced adoption is for you, you can look elsewhere—to older children, handicapped babies, or foreign or private sources. Private adoptions now constitute over half of all adoptions nationwide. Expect to make some difficult choices.

Do your homework. Begin by reading the sections on special-needs and foreign children in Chapter Two of this book. You'll need to think seriously about how an adoption like this might affect your family. Educating yourselves about potential problems can help you succeed with a special adoption.

Despite all the inherent problems, adoption does work. Adopting a child will add an extra dimension to your family, as long as there is a good foundation in your marriage. Repeatedly, couples say adoption makes their marriages and relationships stronger.

Typically, the parents' relationship with an adopted child is every bit as warm, as loving, and as meaningful as are those of people who give birth to their own children. Often adoptive parents are surprised at the fact that the adoptive child so readily becomes "our child."

"On the second day," one couple said in amazement, "it felt like forever."

Once the family is in place, the adoption melts into the background. So if you want to adopt, do. But promise yourself, you will adopt for the right reasons—and with understanding, commitment, and love.

CHAPTER TWO

Understanding the Spectrum of Adoption Services

In this chapter, we will discuss seven paths through the maze of adoption. As with any maze, there can be blind corridors and dead ends, so prepare yourself, and expect the unexpected.

The paths involve *licensed non-profit agencies, for-profit adoption services, independent adoptions, do-it-yourself adoptions, foreign adoptions, special-needs adoptions,* and *relative adoptions.*

Now that you have decided to adopt a child, you're eager to create your new family immediately. Remember: You are not alone. It's estimated that as many as fifty thousand children are adopted each year. Yet, conservative statistics suggest that at least *fifty* times that many people in the United States want to adopt—more than two and a half million of them.

That demand means intense competition for available, healthy babies. And it means you must be thorough, realistic, careful and patient as you sort through your options. You can succeed. But you need to understand the competition—and the system.

First, identify the services available to you. Look in the yellow pages of your phone book under "Adoption" or "Social Services." If you live in a small town or rural community, you'll be more successful if you tap into the resources of the nearest good-size city (preferably in your state, because many services will not work with non-residents).

Remember, whenever you speak to a source, always ask, "Who else should I talk to?"

- Write to the department in your state government that deals with adoption services and ask for a list of those services.
- Write to national organizations and ask for a list of all agencies that serve your area. Be sure to request the listing of any out-of-state organizations licensed to work with you.
- Call the court clerk who works in your state court system dealing with juvenile matters and ask for the court's list of recommended adoption services.
- Contact the referral services in your community and ask them about adoption organizations.

In addition, contact the following:

- Religious organizations for religiously affiliated adoption services.
- Your state bar association for the names of lawyers working in the field of adoption.
- Medical societies for names of doctors who may be involved with adoption.
- Support groups for infertile couples, birth parents, adoptive parents and/or adopted children. Most adoption agencies have access to these groups. Because these groups keep abreast of current trends and resources, they may be very helpful.

The challenge now is to sort through the list, make sure it is inclusive, and then begin the evaluation process. How will you decide which approach is best for you?

The following list will provide research guidelines to help you estimate the pros and cons of the various organizations you contact. Of course, every agency is different; and for every generalization, there is an exception. Honestly consider the types of services for which you would most likely qualify. There is no point pursuing dead ends. If you are unsure, however, by all means ask.

LICENSED, NON-PROFIT AGENCIES

At present, most adoption services in the country fall into this category. They are licensed by the state in which they operate. Non-profit adoption agencies are typically affiliated with an umbrella organization, which provides complementary social services. In other words, adoption usually is only one of many services; others include family counseling, foster care, and substance-abuse counseling.

1. Religiously Affiliated Non-Profit Agencies

These agencies are an outgrowth of the traditional support services offered by church groups and religious organizations. In these agencies, tradition dictates that children should be adopted by religiously compatible parents. However, many religiously affiliated agencies now work with individuals from all backgrounds and do not limit their services to members of their particular religion. When exploring your options, be sure to ask.

Advantages

- These agencies tend to be well established, reputable, and honorably motivated. They have probably been "doing adoptions" for decades; their references can be easily checked.
- If religion is important to you, there is a fair like-

lihood that the baby you adopt will be from your religious background. As the supply of newborns continues to shrink, however, more and more religious organizations are accepting, and even soliciting, babies from birth mothers of other religions.

- Most offer an overall program that includes other services, such as family counseling and foster care.
- If you are an active church member of good standing in your community, and if the church and agency have strong ties and common membership, then it's likely you'll be considered ahead of those who don't belong to your church or synagogue.
- If you are a regular and substantial contributor, so much the better. Some religious agencies may review your gifts and contributions along with your church attendance.
- If your church wants to build its membership in your district, then you may have a good chance of adopting even though you already have one or more children. In most other agencies, parents with children tend to be downgraded because so many couples have no children.
- Usually these agencies can provide financial help for special adoptions through state and federal programs.
- Religious agencies have loyal, built-in referral sources. Pregnancy counseling services, members of the congregation, and other groups all refer birth mothers to the agency's adoption pool.

• Religious agencies almost always have a board of directors that contributes to the agency's support and credibility. Some religious agencies even have national boards that sponsor educational conferences about adoption issues.

• Fees tend to be affordable because they are subsidized by the church or synagogue and various charities. They usually range from about $5,000 to $20,000. Fees are often charged on a sliding scale depending on income level. Also, costs of support services, such as legal and medical fees, may be donated or discounted. But remember that costs vary dramatically depending on the amount and number of charitable contributions to the agency.

Disadvantages

• These organizations tend to be extremely conservative and traditional.

• Agencies can impose specific requirements, and the placement of children can be arbitrary. Often, both husband and wife must be of the same religion, or they must have been married in the church.

Reasons for your rejection can be vague. You haven't been attending services regularly. You are not as supportive of the church as you might be. For whatever reason, your minister, priest or rabbi decides not to recommend you.

Sometimes, if you don't follow up, or fail to make donations, you could be left out in the cold. For all you know, you are still on the list, but nothing happens.

Yet someone who went on the list two years after you has already received a healthy newborn.

• Generally, the philosophy is: "We're not here for the financial gain. Every child is important, and we're going to try to place every needy child who comes to us, regardless of age or situation."

And you might be told, "We have some children who need help. If you don't take this one, there may not be another." Although the objectives are honorable, you may be confronted with a heart-rending choice and encouraged to take a child who is not right for you.

• Congregation members may be awarded preferential treatment; if you're not among that select group, you may be overlooked.

• Your privacy may be compromised. Adoptive parents may fear that others in the congregation will know they are infertile, while the birth mother may not want others in the congregation to know about the adoption. When both the birth mother or birth father and the adoptive parents belong to the same congregation, confidential information may become common knowledge, especially if a newborn is placed with congregation members soon after birth.

• There can be religious pressure on waiting parents. One couple, after waiting fruitlessly on their church list for several years, decided to look elsewhere. They were confronted with: "How can you leave us? You're a member of our congregation. We're going to take care of you!" But the couple had sacrificed precious years to that list and still had no promise of a child.

• A birth mother too young to understand religious fervor may be angry about the adoption as she gets older. "I was told God wanted me to do it," she may say. "When I was sixteen, I didn't know. But I do now. I'm older now, and I want my baby back."

• The legal implications can be serious.

2. Licensed, Non-Profit, Non-Denominational Agencies

These agencies often are affiliated with charitable or quasi-public organizations. They, too, have evolved to fill a need over the years and tend to have a long track record of community service.

Advantages

• Generally, these agencies are open to people from all religious and ethnic backgrounds. You don't have to fit into any particular category to be accepted into their programs. Although some have age and marital-status restrictions, others accept singles, older couples, and couples in mixed marriages or of different religions.

The cost of adoption may vary dramatically depending on the size and scope of the adoption agency program. An organization that provides housing, counseling, medical and legal services and clothing and transportation can justify fees in excess of $20,000. Many agencies are able to charge less because they receive charitable contributions or free services from the community or state. They usually accept birth mothers from all referral sources. Some non-profits, however, specialize in certain types of adoptions, such as children of specific ethnic backgrounds or with special needs. Because their mission is to serve the community, non-profit agencies typically offer many services other than adoption.

Disadvantages

• Generally, the child is considered the client. The agency is in the business of finding the right home for him or her. An adoptive parent needs to be aware of this because it means the agency may encourage the birth mother to keep her baby. Or the agency may put a high priority on placing special-needs children.

• Because many of these agencies operate on a tight budget, they may be slower to modernize. In some cases, they may scrimp on legal advice, which can cause problems.

• In other ways, too, non-profit agencies tend to be highly structured and traditional in their approach, slow to embrace new trends and services. Because the agencies are not in business to make money, most people think their service must be a good one.

• Many non-profit agencies are doing fewer adoptions today because their referral systems have broken down. (On the other hand, a smaller agency, if its list of acceptable adoptive parents is kept small as well, can offer personalized service and care.)

- The wait for a baby tends to be lengthy, often three to seven years, although this can vary enormously.

3. State-Supported Agencies

Most of the children available for adoption through state agencies today have special needs, or are minority or older children. Some have been in foster homes because their biological parents are unable to parent. Others were taken from their families by the courts. Still others are physically or learning disabled. Occasionally, newborns do come into the state's custody: for example, the baby of a birth mother in a foster home.

Some states no longer have services for newborns and turn infants over to private agencies. Other states have so-called life books, in which available children are publicized to interested adoptive parents.

Advantages

- Adoptive parents who don't qualify for other agency lists are eligible if they meet basic qualifications, such as the ability to offer shelter and schooling. (However, those with serious criminal records or a history of substance abuse will probably be disqualified.) Criteria tend to be less restrictive, with emphasis on qualities such as stability and maturity. Singles are readily accepted onto these lists.

• People who can't afford a private agency or lawyer can adopt through a state service. Typically, fees are nominal or waived entirely.

• Those with proven parenting skills who want a special child, a minority, an older child, or a sibling group often are given priority.

• Normally, a state agency can provide support services, although the type and quality vary widely from state to state. Arizona, for example, offers attachment therapy, which helps adopted children understand the adoption process and bond with their adoptive parents.

Disadvantages

• If you want to adopt a perfect, healthy baby, you could be put at the end of a list that numbers into the hundreds and translates into a wait of many years, if such an adoption is possible at all.

• In some cases you may not know much about the background of your adoptive baby's birth parents. In other situations, you may have information about the birth parents, but learn little about your baby's foster parents—and, therefore, his or her care and habits. Of course, there are exceptions.

• There can be a great deal of red tape and inflexibility in the process.

• Here, too, the child is the client. The decision to place hinges on whether a family or individual can meet a child's needs.

National Non-Profit Agencies

Although these agencies closely resemble the other non-profits described in this section, they differ in that they work nationally, across state lines.

Advantages

• These agencies are successful in placing babies for adoption (or they would not have expanded nationwide). They usually work with healthy American babies and, increasingly, healthy foreign babies as well.

• They tend to be highly dependable and predictable, with good track records.

• They typically have a wide range of support services for both the adoptive and birth parents.

• They have developed a strong support group of adoptive parents, grandparents, and birth parents who help them with solicitation across state lines.

Disadvantages

• There are a tremendous number of applicants. Thus, national non-profit agency lists can be highly competitive.

• Fees for national agencies are higher than those for local agencies, typically $10,000 to $25,000, because they are sought out by birth parents who want comprehensive services. Those services are expensive. Watch for add-on fees, also.

• Usually, these agencies have a strong fund-raising component, either in-house or through a foundation.

Adoptive parents are expected to contribute—not only in services, but financially. One national agency will put you on their list only if you agree to become a lifetime fund-raiser for them. This fund-raising aspect can be a plus, of course, in attracting adoptable children and providing services.

• National agencies must comply with regulations of the states in which they operate, so they may not always have the same program from state to state.

FOR-PROFIT ADOPTION SERVICES

LICENSED FOR-PROFIT AGENCIES

As the demand for adoption grows, more for-profit agencies will be opening, but there are still relatively few of these newer agencies, which usually are national in scope.

Advantages

• Because for-profit agencies do not depend on funding with strings attached, they control the type of babies they place and are able to be more flexible in selecting adoptive parents.

• These agencies tend to be more businesslike in their approach and dealings with their clients and licensing organizations. "Traditional adoption options aren't working," is the attitude. "We're going to do things differently."

Because they are not grounded in tradition or by an allegiance to a conservative service organization, for-profit agencies usually are more innovative in their approach to adoption. They must develop their own resources and use creative methods to attract both clients and birth mothers.

Most for-profit agencies offer housing and comprehensive care to birth mothers who need help. At Southwest Adoption Center, Inc., and Adoption Center of Washington, Inc., we ask in-state adoptive parents to house a birth mother (not the birth mother of the child they will adopt) during the last weeks or months of her pregnancy. Not only does this provide a home for the birth mother and expose her to the needs of the adoptive parents, it also helps parents understand the feelings and concerns of a birth mother.

• For-profit agencies are in the business of finding suitable parents for a child. These agencies rarely stray into social service areas such as long-term foster care or substance abuse counseling unless they are related to an adoption. Their programs are set up to meet the needs of the child, birth parents, and adoptive parents in a manner necessary to complete a successful adoption. For-profit agencies tend to specialize in adoption. Because these agencies are typically well financed, they can offer better counseling and comprehensive social services to support their adoption service. Most do so; some don't.

• Most for-profit agencies complete more adoptions than their non-profit counterparts.

• Usually, for-profit agencies accept out-of-state clients.

• For-profit centers are more likely to have a broader range of healthy newborns available for adoption than the more traditional agencies.

• For-profit centers specify what services they can provide and within what period of time.

• Because they are for-profit, these agencies tend to be more closely regulated and reviewed than non-profit agencies. So they are more readily accountable for their practices than are non-profits.

• For-profit agencies are flexible when considering requests from adoptive parents and birth parents who wish to participate in open adoptions or post-adoption exchanges.

Disadvantages

• For-profit agencies are more expensive. Because the agencies are rarely subsidized, adoptive parents are charged fees equal to the average cost of providing an adoption program, plus profits. Costs for doctors, lawyers, care of the birth mother, and overhead, including advertising, are all factored in. Costs average $10,000 to $30,000.

• There remains a suspicion about someone *making money* from adoption, whether it be by a licensed for-profit agency or an attorney. Some individuals and agencies are uncomfortable with this notion. Remember that these for-profit agencies and attorneys must comply with the same licensing standards and court reviews as non-profit agencies.

When contacting a for-profit agency, it also is important to understand that most services provided in an adoption, including the hospital, doctor, and lawyer, are for-profit, too. Ensure that the agency is licensed, or that the attorney is in good standing with the state bar association.

INDEPENDENT ADOPTIONS

Because of the staggering wait at many agencies, and the trend toward open adoptions, the number of private adoptions—those done outside the purview of licensed agencies—has overtaken the number of agency adoptions.

These adoptions are founded on less traditional approaches. They bypass the stream of red tape and strict requirements typically imposed by agencies. The adopters or their intermediaries—lawyers, doctors, or adoption facilitators—locate the babies directly and make all arrangements. Agencies become involved only if their participation is required by state law for completion of a home study (see Chapter Four). For those unqualified to adopt by agency standards, private adoption provides an alternate route to a healthy baby.

Why are there so many independent adoptions? Private adoption lawyers say they sharply reduce the wait by contacting birth mothers more directly than agencies do. Independent adoptions also appeal to birth mothers who want to actively choose their baby's adoptive parents or who do not want to be subject to agency evaluation or go through counseling. Be aware that a number of states do not allow independent adoptions. Check your own state laws to make sure that independent adoption is legal in your state.

1. Lawyer Adoptions

Here we are talking about private attorneys who perform adoptions, not attorneys who happen to run a licensed adoption agency. Essentially, an attorney is retained to find you a baby and/or to legally process an adoption.

Advantages

- The adopting parents are the client and tend to have more control of the process.
- There is no discrimination. An attorney will represent you if you are single or seventy-two years old or physically handicapped. However, many lawyers are involved in open adoptions in which the birth mother and the adoptive parents choose one another.
- If the adoptive couple wants it, there can be a great deal of interaction with the birth parents. Often adoptive parents can meet the birth mother and get direct answers about the baby's background. Sometimes a birth mother can see the home where her baby will live.
- A client can specify the type of baby sought.

• Attorneys may have loyal, consistent referral sources, such as physicians.

• You can tap into the attorney-client privilege for maximum confidentiality. Confidentiality is broken only when the birth father cannot be found and publication is required (see Chapter Six on legal issues).

Generally, you will have more privacy when you adopt through an attorney as opposed to some agencies, which may brief up to 150 prospective adoptive couples together. A lawyer will always meet with his clients privately, if requested.

In New York, a lawyer with a substantial adoption practice says he deals with about five hundred couples a year (40 percent out of state) with an overall success rate of 90 to 95 percent. He advocates self-advertising, a typical approach in private adoptions in which adoptive parents advertise for birth mothers.

A typical lawyer's adoption services include the following: screening birth-mother leads and gathering histories; assisting the birth mother in obtaining medical assistance and providing counseling referrals; handling the disbursement of funds; explaining the legal process, the social worker's role, and the home study; filing the adoption petition, necessary reports, and legal papers; coordinating the adoption plan with the doctor and the hospital.

For those with a specific need or those who have already identified a prospective adoptee, a reputable, adoption-experienced lawyer can be ideal.

Disadvantages

• Any attorney can do adoptions. We tend to assume all attorneys know the law. But adoptions do not fall into a neat legal package. Unless the attorney specializes in adoptions, he or she is unlikely to be aware of the many legal and emotional nuances involved.

• Some states, such as Texas and Minnesota, do not allow private adoptions. In most other states, there is no regulation of adoptions handled by attorneys. That can lead to abuses.

• The lawyer is hired to cut through red tape, to obtain a result. Most lawyers do not look at the long-term effects of the adoption. They are focusing on the legal work, not the social and emotional implications. As a result, needs of the birth parents and the baby tend to be ignored. Often, neither adoptive parents nor birth mothers get sufficient counseling. Many unsuspecting parents do not realize the need for counseling until years later.

A lawyer might say, "My birth mothers don't need counseling. They know what they want." Yet in California, after giving birth, a birth parent may have up to six months to sign the consent-to-adopt forms. During that time, either birth parent may reclaim the baby from the adoptive parents. It can be an enormous gamble, especially in a case where the birth mother has not dealt with adoption issues through professional counseling.

• There may be inadequate information available regarding the birth parents. Although most states require a medical and social history for every adoption, many lawyers obtain only minimal information. As long as the legal documents are correctly filed with the court, the lawyer, unlike most agencies, may not make a real search for the birth father's medical and social history.

• The birth father often is ignored. "Don't worry about the father," you might hear. "We'll take care of that legally."

The birth father might not even know the baby exists. But if he finds out, it could pose a legal risk that could cause an adoption to be overturned.

• Costs vary because the adoptive parents are responsible for the lawyer's fees as well as the bills for the birth mother. An average adoption fee for a lawyer is $2,000 to $6,000. Add to that $3,000 to $20,000 for the birth mother's medical costs, a wild card that can create chaos. What if the birth mother has a Caesarean section and needs intensive care? What if the baby is premature, incurring bills at the rate of $2,000 a day? Women who receive no prenatal care are three times more likely to deliver low-birthweight babies. Low-birthweight babies, as a general rule, need extensive medical care. Bills for premature babies *average* $30,000, and can go much higher.

• What if the birth mother decides to keep her baby? In independent adoptions, you may have to guarantee the doctor and hospital bills. Birth parents may not repay you for these costs, even if they keep the child after the birth. And you'll have to cope with the incredible letdown and emotional trauma. You have done an enormous amount of work to locate that baby, and you have invested emotionally in "your" birth mother and her baby.

Working through an attorney may not result in the placement of a child, and you probably still owe your lawyer his fee, regardless of the outcome.

2. Physician Adoptions

Occasionally, a doctor who is doing infertility counseling, gynecology and infant delivery arranges adoptions as a byproduct of his practice. He or she may have a core of counselors and a formalized program or, more often, an informal, sporadic adoption practice that is dependent on supply. Sometimes, he'll work with a private attorney to whom he refers these cases for legal help.

Advantages

• Doctors are likely to come across birth mothers interested in discussing adoption. Mention your interest in adopting to your doctor. You may also want to call or write gynecologists in your yellow pages and ask whether they are involved in adoption.

Disadvantages

• Fees are variable. Some doctors do not charge for their roles in adoption; others charge more than agencies or attorneys.

• Physicians usually know no more about adoption

than anyone else. Most know little about the need for counseling, the legal ramifications of adoption, or the matching process. Delivering babies has little in common with arranging adoptions. Physicians are not licensed adoption agencies; nor are they licensed to practice law. Doing an adoption through a physician may be illegal, if you do not enlist the help of an attorney or licensed adoption agency.

• Often, it's a take-it-or-leave-it situation. When adopting through a doctor, adoptive parents usually have little choice among babies. At best, there may be one or two children available, so a match selected from a variety of choices is unlikely.

• Physicians rarely make plans for the sick or handicapped child. Compare this to a licensed adoption agency, which has access to many potential adoptive couples when a special-needs child is born. Without adequate counseling, an adoptive parent may feel obligated to pay for large medical bills and adopt a child who needs special care.

A physician who is not adequately trained in the specialized area of adoptions may inadvertently contribute to poor adoption practices. Post-adoption exchange of picture and other information, counseling, and post-adoption support groups are seldom, if ever, initiated by a physician.

DO-IT-YOURSELF ADOPTIONS

Frustrated by the wait or the scarcity of healthy newborns or their inability to measure up to the ideal parent profile, many people are turning to private methods to supplement their attempts at adopting through agencies or to supplant them altogether.

If you adopt through private or informal methods, be certain you understand the downside. Risks are not inconsequential. If you find a baby through private sources, you will have to arrange for the state-mandated studies and reports and hire a lawyer to finalize the legal work.

You can find babies through the following informal sources or with the help of a formal adoption facilitator.

1. Informal Sources

These sources are not actually in the adoption business. However, they are involved in some way in the adoption field and can serve as informal referral networks.

• Social workers. They are not set up as formal counselors to locate babies, but they work in the adoption field and can send you in the most promising directions.

• Physicians. They fall into this category if they are not involved with a formal adoption service. Be sure to talk to those working with the doctors as well: nurses, assistants, receptionists, secretaries, even accountants.

- Active members in your religious community. This includes pastors, ministers, rabbis, priests, as well as their staffs and volunteers.
- Other counselors, particularly those who work with pregnant women in programs such as Planned Parenthood and pro-life groups.
- Individuals in the education system who come in contact with birth mothers. These would be school nurses, school counselors, etc.
- Support groups for adoptive parents at organizations such as the Open Door Society. You can get first-hand referrals, as well as meet other successful adoptive parents.
- Therapists, psychologists, and psychiatrists. They may be able to refer you to a valid source.
- Your friends. They themselves may have adopted, or they may know of someone wanting to place a baby. Don't be shy. Ask everyone you know. Word of mouth is remarkably effective. Once you begin to explore, you will be amazed at the numbers of people who have been touched by adoption.

2. Adoption Facilitators

Facilitators offer some of the same services as agencies, but they are primarily geared to help you find available babies. Many of these services are run by adopters frustrated by the traditional system; they want to help others circumvent the red tape. If you decide to use a facilitator, be sure to get supplemental counseling and legal support.

Adoption facilitators are consultants, period. (Generally, support systems and counseling programs are not included and must be contracted for separately.) Often the services will provide a list of contacts or at least sources of contacts. They will tell you how to write a resumé to attract birth mothers, how to write advertisements filled with pathos and love, and how to construct photographs so they have the most appeal. Generally, they will guide you in an advertising and direct-mail campaign, as do many adoption lawyers. There also is usually an education component, a reading list or adoption seminars.

This is an expanding field that is relatively unregulated, so be wary of differing levels of experience and expertise and a greatly varying ability to provide results. Prices vary substantially, from several hundred dollars to several thousand. Generally, fees are charged for each item and almost never include the significant costs of the required advertising and direct-mail campaigns; medical and birth-mother support costs, such as housing, counseling, and transportation; and legal fees.

Be aware that doing your own advertising and mailing can be expensive. Some adoptive couples send out over two thousand resumés. At a conservative estimate, calculate fifteen minutes to mail every resumé because you must locate the source and address the letter. This can be over five hundred hours of your time. Once the letters are sent you will want to respond to birth-parent contacts. This can be hugely time-consuming, particularly when most leads do not pan out.

Adoption consultants often promote cooperative adoptions—that is, adoptions in which birth parents and adoptive parents have full knowledge of one another. A cooperative adoption counselor may facilitate several hundred adoptions per year in a state such as California.

In carefully supervised and supported agency adoptions, the placement rate—the number of birth mothers who opt for adoption and who actually place their babies—is said to be less than 50 percent. A birth mother who has received minimal counseling and support is even less likely to go through with the adoption. Be certain that "your" birth mother has received counseling and understands her options before you commit.

Typically, a couple interested in a cooperative approach will do extra reading from a reading list weighted heavily toward cooperative adoption.

If you agree with the open-adoption approach outlined in the readings, you move on to the next step and subscribe to a cooperative approach, as ensuring an ongoing relationship among the child and both the adoptive and the birth parents. In one recent case, the adoptive parents went to the hospital with the birth mother when she gave birth, then took the birth mother home to live with them for the next two months. The adoption was completed, and the birth mother remains friendly with the adoptive family.

Some adoptive families may mail 1,500 to 2,000 resumés—including an essay and pictures—to the birth-mother sources, such as doctors, hospitals, social workers, and school nurses. In turn, many birth mothers will call up as many as seventy-five to eighty prospective adopters. If you choose this approach, begin the process at least six months before you are ready to accept a baby into your home.

It is important that you ask questions about fees. Understanding how they are determined can help you avoid being victimized and to be realistic about lawyers' fees in your state. You should know that you will be making some difficult choices and that you are entitled to make them carefully. Take as much time as you need to investigate your options and make your decisions. Realize that you can say no and that there will still be another baby for you.

3. Advertising/Direct Mail

You can do this with the help of a facilitator as outlined in section 2 or on your own. The following are typical of advertisements for private adoptions:

"Young couple wishes to give child beautiful home, much love and security he or she so deserves. Strictly legal, confidential."

"Happily married couple unable to have baby desires to adopt newborn. Can give warmth, love, security, confidentiality. Call collect."

"A sunny nursery awaits your baby. We offer a beautiful home, family travel, summers in the country, loving grandparents, cousins, and 'The Best Things in Life.' "

"Full heart and empty nursery. Give your baby a happy, secure future. All our love, good income, a warm professional home with books & music and summers at the ocean await your newborn."

"We know this is a very difficult decision for you. We promise to provide the love, warmth and security your baby needs. We are a loving, financially secure couple, active in scouting, athletic and church activities. Large home w/backyard, stay-at-home mother."

With or without the assistance of a placement service, more people are advertising to find a baby, and advertising and direct-marketing campaigns are increasingly sophisticated.

Advertisements are showing up everywhere: on bus-stop benches, on billboards, in doctors' offices, on television, in foreign journals. If you're not extremely cautious, you can be opening yourself up to huge legal and emotional risks. One recent ad from a "well educated" couple promised "all expenses plus." Make sure that your ad doesn't say, in effect, "I'm willing to take a baby from absolutely anyone. And I'll pay whatever it takes." It's illegal to *buy* a baby.

If you feel certain background is important, you may want to target your ads, say to all the college newspapers in your region if you want a college mother, or to Catholic publications, if you are seeking Catholic birth parents.

Advertisements for babies interspersed among personal ads in college newspapers are popular, but not necessarily productive. Many are flooded with ads, yet one college reports only two known adoptions in eight years. You may decide to advertise in junior-college publications, where there is less competition, or in vocational and trade-school newsletters.

Some states prohibit advertising altogether, others outlaw certain types of ads. And many publications refuse to accept any adoption ads. You are responsible for knowing the law.

Most private campaigns include a combination of advertisements and direct mailings with pictures and resumés to adoption resources.

Include a picture, a brief introduction, the length of your marriage, a description of your home and other family members. It should be very basic—most birth parents will spend only a few seconds looking at it. Sending three hundred or so should be sufficient to find a baby within six months to a year.

Advertising/Direct Mail Follow-up

One of your first considerations should be protecting your privacy. Even if you ultimately decide in favor of open adoption, it makes sense to arrange for a special telephone line, reserved exclusively for responses to your ads, so every caller does not have your personal phone number. Better, have your lawyer or counselor screen calls to qualify callers initially.

When you receive a call, think it through. Why did

the birth mother call you instead of an adoption service? Why is she circumventing the system? Is she after money? Does she think there is something the matter with her baby? Is she worried about her privacy? Does she want to control the situation by choosing her baby's parents herself?

Many birth mothers want an open adoption. Is that acceptable to you? She may sound so happy to talk to you, so trustworthy and loving.

"I have to meet you to know you are right for my baby," she might say. "I'll never come back for my baby."

Few birth mothers do come back. But you must be comfortable with the implications of an open adoption in which there is communication between adoptive and birth parents.

You must also evaluate the birth mother carefully. How do you ensure that her baby would be a good match for you?

Most people, in their excitement and relief, say, "I've finally found someone willing to give up her baby."

What if the baby has a birth defect? What if the birth mother asks you about your intentions if the baby isn't healthy? She doesn't want to hear you say that it depends, that you are only interested in a completely healthy baby, that if the baby is impaired, you won't keep it. The answer she wants is that you'll treat her baby as your baby and do whatever is necessary, that you'll take full responsibility. What happens if you respond that way and your worst fears are realized? What if you see the baby and realize you simply can't follow through?

Or suppose you have paid support, all prenatal care, and guaranteed the hospital and medical bills. What happens if the birth mother calls you and says, "I've changed my mind. I think I'll keep my baby."

Are you prepared for this very real possibility? Are you willing to take the risk?

It's also possible the birth mother will call and say, "I'm in the hospital with my baby. I'm thinking of keeping her. But I really need more money. Can you pay me $3,000 more?"

What then? That is illegal. But would you report her? You might reason that because you've gone so far, paying a little more won't matter, especially since your dream of a family might finally become a reality.

What if she comes back to you later, asking for still more money? She could threaten to say you paid her to give up her baby, even if you have done everything by the book. Or if you live in California, where she may not sign a consent-to-adopt form for up to six months after her baby has been placed with you, she could come back again and again.

Remember, you have little recourse in situations like these. Even when the law is broken, how likely are you to recover costs—even if you are willing to go to court?

In a worst-case scenario, a pregnant woman might answer your ad and gain your financial support without ever intending to give up her baby. There was one case in which a single birth mother managed to get money from six sets of adopters. Most birth mothers are decent women who would never knowingly abuse the law. But there are exceptions.

The birth mother is as vulnerable in these situations as the adopter. What assurance does she have that you are who you say you are? You have not been validated by an agency (although all adoptive parents must be recommended in a home study by a designee of their state).

A California adoption attorney contends that it is in the interest of a birth mother to conclude a satisfactory adoption for her baby.

"Someone is taking her baby and setting her free," he says. In fact, he argues, the birth mother has more to gain than the adoptive parents because she "needs someone to adopt more than someone needs to adopt."

He suggests a birth mother is a poor risk if, in her discussion with you or your representative, she says something along the following lines:

- "Don't worry, I won't change my mind."
- "Is there any payment?"
- "It's not fair that the man goes free and I have to suffer."

These are statements that focus on the mother's problems not what is best for the child.

He says that the birth mother who sincerely wants

to place her baby won't talk about changing her mind or getting paid.

"The woman who will go through with an adoption prioritizes her baby," he says. "If she doesn't show up for appointments, if she doesn't sign papers right away, if she acts as if she is doing you a favor, it means she doesn't value adoption."

Despite the risks, independent and self-directed adoptions are, indeed, successful. In fact, they now make up the majority of all U.S. adoptions. Many people who would not be able to adopt otherwise are succeeding through private means. However, with more and more people trying this route, it is taking longer—up to several years.

Before committing to private or do-it-yourself methods, do your homework. Know your risks. Read everything about the subject you can locate (see Information Guide at the back of this book). And only participate armed with legal assistance and counseling.

FOREIGN ADOPTIONS

More than ten thousand people adopted foreign children last year. Almost all were from Third World countries, since most developed countries—especially those in Western Europe—are experiencing a baby deficit similar to our own.

Challenges include the tremendous volume of paperwork, the difficulty of identifying reputable, reliable adoption services, the health risks, the logistics of international dealings, and the implications of raising a baby with racial and cultural differences.

Advantages

Despite those obstacles, here are some reasons to consider foreign adoption:

- You want a family, and you feel children are the same the world over.
- You want a child as quickly as possible. The wait for a healthy newborn can be much shorter than in the United States.
- You may be unable to adopt an American baby but feel strongly that you want to adopt as young a child as possible.
- You choose to adopt overseas to minimize the perceived risk of birth-parent interference later in the child's life.
- You can't afford the fees of an American adoption. Foreign adoptions *can* be less expensive; they may be subsidized by a church or international adoption group.
- You want to adopt a child from a specific country. We Americans traditionally adopt victimized children from war-torn countries.
- You might think, "We have so much. We can share with people who are not as lucky as we are."

Before making your decision, study, read, and talk with experienced people. There are many support organizations. Attend their meetings; meet with others who have adopted from the countries you are considering.

Considerations

- Are you willing to provide ties to your child's culture, and is it feasible to do so?
- How will your family and friends react?

If you have any reason to think that your friends or family might not accept a foreign child, you may want to reconsider. It takes a special family with a good support network to adopt a foreign child and be sensitive to the needs of his or her heritage.

Once decided, you have three choices:

1. Adopt through an agency that specializes in foreign adoptions.
2. Adopt through an intermediary, perhaps an attorney specializing in international adoptions, or a church or a group with ties to an overseas orphanage.
3. If you are knowledgeable, persistent, and brave enough, do it yourself.

It's best, however, to work with a proven, credible agency that commonly handles foreign adoptions.

Many agencies are turning to overseas sources, and their expertise can be invaluable.

Regardless of your approach, be sure to get answers to the following questions before making a commitment:

- With whom will we be dealing?
- How long will it take?
- How much will it cost? How much money is required up front? What about unexpected expenses? What is the breakdown of fees? Here are the costs you'll probably be responsible for:
  1. Agency fee
  2. Translations
  3. Attorney fees
  4. Additional medical costs
  5. Authentication, documentation and other fees
  6. Birth country lawyer and court costs
  7. Donation to orphanage
  8. Transportation
- Are there any guarantees? Who takes responsibility for unsuccessful placements?
- Can we recover our money if we do not receive a child?
- What type of information will we have about our child?
- What assurances do we have regarding the baby's health?
- What age will our child be?
- What legalities are involved and what will our responsibilities be?

- What is the source of the children? Directly from the birth mother, an agency, a licensed orphanage, other?
- Do children have valid, legal releases from their birth parents or certificates of abandonment?
- What qualifications for adopters apply? For example, South Korea—the source of many foreign adoptees—insists that parents be no more than forty years older than the child they are adopting. Other countries, such as Brazil, consider maturity an asset.
- What is your percentage of disrupted adoptions? What are the causes?
- Whom can we talk to in the United States who have adopted children through you? (This is invaluable.)

Disadvantages

• Because it takes time to process a foreign adoption, you will almost never adopt a newborn, a child in his or her first month of life.

• You may not know what type of emotional bonding has occurred between the baby and the caretaker. Has your baby been in a nursery with fifty others? Or has he or she been in a foster-care situation? Who pays for the care while you are waiting?

• You may not know whether the baby is legally free for adoption. Trafficking in stolen children and fake documents is big business in a number of developing countries.

• Records are frequently nonexistent. You may

never be sure about a child's genetic or social ancestry, let alone his medical history.

• You may receive incorrect information about the health of your baby, which is the single most important consideration in foreign adoptions. The agency might say, "Of course, your baby is fine. We have the doctor's stamp to prove it." Remember, though, that stamp may be a perfunctory one, given by an overworked doctor who cannot spend much time with the seventy-five or one hundred children assigned to him each day. Try to find out whether your baby has received any medical care up to the time of the adoption and the baby's current physical and mental condition.

Before you accept your baby—especially in a private adoption—have him or her examined by a doctor whom you, not the agent, have chosen. If you are not allowed to do this, it's virtually an admission that something is wrong. Of course, usually just by looking, you can tell if your baby is sick. What you don't know is how serious it may be. It is not uncommon to find thrush; a childhood fungus; malnutrition; jaundice; or clubfoot.

• Costs can soar if you are not dealing with an agency that enumerates every fee. When you are discussing fees, whether with an agency or a mediator, or on your own, be certain the fees to all people involved along the way are included. Compute the cost of each step. For instance, if you travel to pick up your baby, are you prepared to manage from two weeks to three months in a foreign country?

• You may have a hard time deciding which country you want to target for a child to adopt. In recent years, the overwhelming majority of foreign adoptees have come from Asia, mostly from South Korea. The second-most-common source is Latin America, with about a third of those children coming from Colombia.

Other countries with a significant number of adoptions include the Philippines, India, Chile, Guatemala, El Salvador, Honduras, and Mexico.

• The paperwork is voluminous and exacting. If you fail to obtain one stamp or do not have enough copies of a particular document, if you have neglected to have some of your papers translated, or if you process in the wrong order, you can jeopardize your entire adoption.

Once you have made your decision, begin gathering your support papers immediately. Arrange for a home study (see Chapter Four). In the United States, initiate the pre-filing process (Advance Processing Application) with the Immigration and Naturalization Service well ahead of time. Usually, your papers will remain valid for at least a year.

Do not fail to do exactly what is required. You are responsible for knowing the requirements and for fulfilling them. Remember that there are many places to turn for help, if you need it. And keep in mind that tens of thousands before you have successfully negotiated the maze.

• You may not have adequate insurance coverage.

Explain to your insurer that, although you will have total responsibility for your baby, the adoption will not be completed when the child arrives in the United States. Often, it takes at least six months to finish the adoption. Find out what is necessary to insure your baby on arrival and establish whether both diagnosed and undiagnosed medical conditions are covered.

Do not accept a "no coverage" response as gospel. Many insurance companies have vague policies concerning adoption. You may have to go up the ladder until you find someone who can make policy for the company as to when the baby falls under your coverage as a dependent. Typically, most insurance companies start coverage when the parents sign the consent to adopt and the child is placed in your home. The adoption court hearing is not the date coverage begins in most cases.

• If you adopt an older child, you may feel burdened by the prospect of learning his customs, what foods he eats, whether religion is a significant part of his life.

• If you adopt privately, you may not have any recourse if things go wrong.

For example, it could cost more than you expect because of payoffs you need to make to lawyers, judges, and immigration officials to get out of the country with your baby. Payoffs in America are against the law, but they are a way of life in many other countries. What happens if someone catches you making a payoff? *You must know the rules of the foreign country where you are adopting.*

Points to Remember after Your Foreign Child Comes to Live with You

• Because of delays, your baby may arrive months older than you expected. Most children—even if they've bonded previously to someone else—make an excellent adjustment.

• Foreign babies can weigh less than American-born babies and appear developmentally delayed. There may be minor correctable problems: undernutrition, parasites, ear, eye or skin infections. There is always the possibility of an undiagnosed or unforeseen medical problem. "Healthy" is a relative term, with U.S. standards optimum. Age estimates may be wrong.

• The orphanage may desire follow up documentation, such as pictures and medical and social profiles as the child grows. This is, in part, a throwback to the days when children were sent abroad as servants. Pictures and gifts for the orphanage are welcome and help ease the way for those who follow, because they reassure the orphanage personnel that adoptive parents care.

• You can work through your problems and questions with parents in a support group who share your experience, especially those who have adopted from the same country as you and from the same orphanage. Your child, as he or she grows, will get invaluable support from peers in the group.

• If your child is older, he may react to the new abundance in life by hoarding food or belongings or by giving everything away. He may need to be taught to care for himself and his or your belongings.

- Keep a scrapbook for him with as much information as you can gather about him.

If your child wants to forget his country of birth, be sure it is not because of feelings of inferiority or because he feels different and disconnected. Inevitably, there will be periods of adjustment—obviously, some more pronounced than others. If there are none, look for reasons. One particularly quiet, accommodating little girl was found to be deaf in one ear.

Obviously, adopting from a foreign land is complex; it has implications for all future generations of your family. But those who have done it compare it to giving birth—painful but absolutely worth it for the joy and fulfillment gained.

SPECIAL-NEEDS ADOPTIONS

Special-needs adoptions include all children who are considered difficult to place. These may range from black babies, for whom there are not enough black adoptive parents, and older children of all races, to children with emotional, mental, and physical handicaps.

Why would you adopt a special-needs child? Because you fall in love with one. Because you are unable to adopt an infant and you have extra patience and persistence. Because you have special training. Because you want to contribute. Because you have the strength, resources, sense of humor, and love essential to these adoptions.

Considerations

• Do you have a united front? Are some family members vehemently opposed? Will they try to disrupt the adoption or cause you extra problems?

• The disruption rate is high—20 to 30 percent according to most sources. And that is the figure for adoptions that don't work after completion, after the adoptive parents have had time to grow into the adoption.

• Will your community accept the adoption? If not, do you have extra resources to help you through this?

• Have you identified professional resources to help assist you?

• Are you and your spouse in full agreement? Do you both have the same amount of information? Are you doing it for the same reasons?

• Are you being coerced into this type of adoption by a well-meaning social worker, especially if you seem to be vacillating? After all, special-needs children are the very hardest to place. If you don't adopt them, who will?

In addition, in most cases, these children are caught up in the welfare system. Their caseworkers want them placed in a permanent home, as do the states.

- Are you flexible? Can you drop everything and respond to a crisis or a need?
- Do you have patience, a high tolerance for frustration?
- Do you have a sense of humor?
- Are you willing to be an advocate for your child? If he isn't getting appropriate help, will you fight for him? Will you be his ally?
- Do you have other child-care experience?
- Can you afford it?

Special-needs children require extra time, energy, and money for counseling, programs to meet their particular requirements for leading lives as normal as possible, medical expenses, and special education. They also need extra love, patience, compassion, and strength.

Do not feel guilty if you decide against adopting a special-needs child. *No one has the right to push you into this decision.*

Generally, the most successful special adoptions involve children with problems you can see. You may not know what those visible problems will mean to your life, but you know there are real problems. There is no pretending.

Almost always, with special-needs children, you have a honeymoon period, a time when your child shows signs of sweetness, accommodation, and responsiveness. You may believe you are so magical that, just by being around you, this child has overcome all problems.

In truth, your child is holding his breath. Feelings of alienation, low self-esteem, and rejection may all be there, waiting to burst forth once his attention is diverted from the newness of you.

Something you did for all the right reasons can end up tearing you and your family apart.

There are special people who can happily manage special adoptions, people who can give abundantly without any need for a return on their investment. Some will spend the rest of their lives nurturing a handicapped child instead of institutionalizing him. But many adoptive parents are not special in that way. Few are prepared to sideline their lives for the sake of a special-needs child.

Locating a Special-Needs Child

There are many available special-needs children. The challenge is to find *your* child and then negotiate the red tape required in state adoptions. Much depends on the state in which you adopt, the agency you adopt through, and the social workers involved.

There are growing numbers of reputable agencies, state organizations, and liaison groups that facilitate such adoptions. There are local, state, regional and national adoption exchanges that act as matching services. Many keep life books, with a picture and some information about each available child.

In certain states, adoption organizations are required by law to list waiting children in their state's exchange book, if they fail to find a home for a child within a prescribed time. In New York, where such a law exists, at least several thousand children are featured every year. Do not expect, however, to find infants or toddlers.

Often, you can register with your state exchange as well as those of other states. Look at the photo-listing books of your state and those nearby on a frequent basis because they are updated regularly. Other sources include newspaper features, television programs, parent groups and organizations that specialize in the particular type of special-needs child you have decided to adopt.

Social workers, agencies, and the states responsible try to make it easy for you to be exposed to these children. In New York, at least two conferences are held each year where social workers from various organizations show slides of available children. Interested adopters check off ballots and register on the spot for the children who appeal to them.

1. Legal-Risk Adoptions

Sometimes called foster adoption, this is a relatively new program that moves children into adoptive homes while legal action continues to free the child for adoption. Many begin as foster-care placements and, because the foster parents want to adopt, develop into a legal-risk adoption. The risk is that you will be taking care of a child who may never become legally free for adoption.

2. Transracial Adoptions

Transracial adoptions are included in this section because they, too, require more from you—more homework, more attention, more understanding.

The overriding issues in these adoptions are ones of identity. You must be comfortable with your child's heritage and offer him an opportunity to learn about his background. Your challenge is to deal with your child so that he accepts you for what you are and still identifies with his heritage.

You can aid in this process by:

• Offering your child ongoing opportunities to learn about his background. Some parent groups sponsor culture camps for various ethnic groups. Others offer year-round programs and newsletters. You also will meet people in situations like yours in these groups.

• Exploring resources available to you. At the least, subscribe to newsletters, read books, seek out others of similar backgrounds. Network. Try to make certain your child has friends of similar backgrounds.

• Consider the adoption of a second or third child with a different heritage as well. Your transracial adoptees do not need to share the same background. When you adopt more than one transracial child, the message to your children becomes, "There is a bunch of us here struggling for the same thing. We're in this together, sharing the same kinds of problems."

Once your child is of school age, he will need help in answering questions so that he feels comfortable with his classmates and friends. Help him understand his background and appreciate the fact that what may be different about him is not a negative.

3. Adoption of Older Children

Generally, any child over two years old is considered an older child for the purposes of adoption. Make no mistake. Older children are not merely big kids. These children are already human beings with life experiences, experiences that have nothing to do with you and to which you probably cannot relate.

By definition, an older, adoptable child has accumulated problems. Otherwise, he wouldn't be free for adoption. These children need a much higher investment than normal. As parents, you need to be:

- Child-centered, committed to focusing a lot of your energy on rearing your child.
- Prepared to be an advocate for your child. Some people can be extremely judgmental and ill-informed.
- Prepared to try to gain access to all available and appropriate community, government, and medical resources.
- Willing to commit extraordinary time and endure substantial, ongoing stress.
- Comfortable with being different as a family.
- Prepared to go on indefinitely, perhaps forever,

understanding that all of your emotional energy may never be reciprocated.

- Willing to give up the idea that your child will ever be a normal, fully functional person. Depending on his personality and the upheavals in his earlier life, he may never recover. Sometimes, despite all of your love and any treatment he receives, your child will end up in an institution or another program.

Considerations

Before succumbing to the appeal of a particular child, find out all you can. Realize that when you first meet him, he's probably on his best behavior. Ask yourself, why is this twelve-year-old child available for adoption? What is it in his background that put him into this position? And how does it affect him?

Once you decide to adopt an older child, learn as much as you can about him. Interview any professional who has dealt with him, as well as any foster parents, his birth parents, the social worker assigned to his case, his teachers, or anyone else who may know him.

The older the child the more experiences he has had—and the more information you will have. If he is three years old, he probably hasn't lived many places. He hasn't been to school and he probably doesn't have many friends yet. If he is older, you have more to go on. How is he doing in school? How does he react to other people? Are there problems in a particular class? Talk to his teachers as well as his caseworkers, and to the people he lives with now and with whom he lived in the past. If you have lived a relatively sheltered, traditional life, some of the problems may shock you.

As ties with his past—his parents, siblings perhaps, neighborhood friends, and community—are severed, the child, who tends to think everything that happens is his fault, is very likely overwhelmed by negative feelings: guilt, rejection, abandonment, loss and anger. Trust is usually a scarce commodity with older children, who have little—if any—sense of belonging or mattering to anyone.

One three-year-old South Korean girl kept asking her adoptive mother, "Did they send me away because I was bad?" Her mother would assure her each time by pulling out a letter from her former foster mother and reading the part that said, "Soo Mee is a lovely child who brings lots of joy to all of us."

"That always made me feel better," says Soo Mee, now a teen-ager.

It is generally agreed that any older child suffers a loss when he is adopted, no matter what the situation is before the adoption. As a result, many professionals believe he experiences, at least to some degree, the predictable states of grief that follow any severe loss—denial, anger, bargaining, depression, and hopefully, acceptance.

Some people compare adopting an older child to getting married. There is an initial attraction and then the reality settles in.

It is best to know one another before committing fully. A pre-adoption plan might include your seeing the child in a setting where he doesn't know you are watching. If you are still positive about him, arrange trips to the zoo, weekend visits at your home, and phone calls and letters. You can both think about how you like each other. Do not be rushed. Take your time.

How will you choose a child? Try to match common interests. If you teach boxing to junior-high children, and you are thinking of adopting a tough twelve-year-old, it might be perfect. If you are a gentle, restrained couple, you might settle on a quieter child. Realize your limits. You do not want to be challenged beyond your capacity.

Have no doubts. There will be problems. They may have to do with withdrawal or extreme shyness or withholding of affection. Or they may be worse. As you inquire about your child, ask everyone, "What were the problems?" "What are the problems now?" "What else should I know?"

For many, there is deep satisfaction in taking a difficult child and helping him become a responsible adult.

Adoption of Mentally or Physically Delayed or Handicapped Children

Often children are both mentally and physically disabled. Their handicaps can range from slight to severe. Without a doubt, these are the most challenging children. Adopting one can fill your life with a sense of accomplishment for loving and parenting such a child. It also can place an enormous burden on you.

Medical Information

Get all that you can. Know what problems to anticipate and ask each expert you consult to play out in detail the best and worst scenarios re:

What will this handicap mean to us?

- How will it change our life?
- How should we prepare ourselves for this child?
- What will it be like in one year, in three years, in five, ten, fifteen, twenty, during the child's adult years?
- How much will it cost?
- What treatment is available now and in the future? Where will we get the treatment? How often will it be necessary? For how long a period?
- Is it correctable? *A big question.* A cleft palate, a clubfoot, certain mental illnesses can be cured readily. You will be surprised what is curable and correctable. Educate yourself further. Read. Talk to parents of children with similar handicaps. Your doctor and/or your adoptive-parent group will help you understand what you are committing to.

Considerations

- Caring for a disabled child can be a lot of physical work.
- Improvement can be in slow, tiny steps with many stumbles along the way. There may be no improvement at all. There may be deterioration.

- Friends may not understand. However, you will find support from other families who have adopted similar children.
- As an adoptive parent, you don't carry the guilt that often accompanies a birth parent of such a child. You can be objective. You have chosen this child.
- Children with severe problems need not be adopted quickly. Again, take your time. Ease into it. See how it feels over longer periods. What about your family? Can they handle it? Do they want to? If you have other children, it can be embarrassing to have a sibling who looks and/or acts differently at school. What demands will be made on the healthy siblings?

If you are thinking of adopting a child with a severe condition, consider volunteering at a hospital or health center. You will find out what it is like to care for such a child. In fact, nurses or doctors or other professionals who are exposed to a particular handicap or child often adopt. They are likely to focus on the individual child and look beyond the handicap.

Financial assistance is frequently available to help underwrite the costs of caring for a handicapped child. In many states, there are tax advantages as well.

If you adopt a special-needs child, tap into every available resource—especially the special-parent groups. You'll be able to talk freely about what is happening at your house and get not only sympathy and understanding, but solid advice as well.

Parents who adopt the most severely handicapped children tend to have the fewest disruptions. Apparently, they realize any substantive change in the child's condition is unlikely. And they realize, as you should, that such a child probably would not be doing as well in another, non-adoptive environment.

Locating a Mentally or Physically Handicapped Child

- If you see a child who interests you in a state or private-agency listing book, call, don't write. You may be too late.
- Remember, the photo-listing books are updated regularly, so check them often.
- Follow up on more than one child at a time.
- List yourself with as many exchanges as possible. You never know where your child may be.
- Track your queries and follow up yourself at the appointed time. Do not wait for agencies to call you back. Remember the overload factor. Always note whom you talk with, the date, and any information about each child.
- If you are turned down, ask why.
- Be persistent.

With all special-needs adoptions, most successful are the couples and individuals who carve out time for themselves away from their children and keep perspective and balance in their lives.

Many people are not able to carry through a special-needs adoption. But some of you can. Consider it. If you are among those who can parent a special-needs child, do it. There are so many waiting for someone like you.

RELATIVE ADOPTIONS

A high percentage of all adoptions in the United States involves family members. Because this book is devoted to helping those without such sources, we will not spend much time discussing these adoptions.

However, we urge all of you involved in relative adoptions to read the remainder of our book carefully because adoption issues are just as important for family members as they are for strangers. The need for counseling is every bit as urgent. In fact, family adoptions can be overlaid with even more emotional concerns than third-party adoptions.

In many cultures, there's enormous pressure to keep a child in the family, rather than give him or her up to strangers. If a cousin, a married sister, or even the parents of a birth mother will adopt her child, it's a happy solution to a family crisis.

Despite the pressures involved, in certain situations the child might be better off financially and emotionally outside the family. Certainly, that possibility should be explored.

CHAPTER THREE

Finding the Agency That's Right for You

You have done your initial homework. You are committed to adoption. You have considered the different approaches and thought carefully about the type of baby you'd like to adopt. Suppress the temptation to sign with the first agency that accepts you onto their waiting list. Remember, nothing less than your future and your family are at stake. Knowledge is control. The more you know going in, the more sure the result. The more thorough you are at this stage, the more rewarding your adoption. And the more peace you'll have during the inevitable wait.

This chapter will help you through seven basic steps for finding the right agency. They involve: *developing your personal criteria, including your preferences for closed, open, or cooperative adoptions; writing the initial query letters; developing and completing agency checklists; evaluating the agency's written information; interviewing an agency representative; interviewing other sources, including references, for additional information;* and *deciding on your short list of agencies.* (For the sake of simplicity, we use "agency" to mean any adoption-placement organization.)

As you work through this process, keep in mind that all agencies are inundated with queries. Virtually all operate on overload. And understand that no two agencies are alike.

Some agencies will be willing to respond to your questions by telephone, some in writing. Others will require a personal interview or ask you to participate in one or more orientation sessions. Many organizations require you to pay an up-front fee for the answers you seek.

Regardless, the best approach is to write the agency. The agency may offer many other services in addition to adoption. You do not want to risk your future on a person who does not specialize in adoption but who happens to answer the phone. Maybe he or she has three other calls on hold. Perhaps the person is a temporary or a new employee, with insufficient—or worse—incorrect information.

Write a brief letter expressing your interest in adoption and ask the following:

1. "Will you please send me all your written materials?"

2. "How can I acquire additional information about your adoption services and process?"
3. Whom should I contact to discuss my questions further?"

Now you need to evaluate the organization you will depend on for your adoption. We suggest you use two checklists: one with our categories and one with your own criteria.

Make up a sheet with your criteria along the left margin. As you evaluate each agency, write its name across the top and compare it with the others against each criterion. Complete your checklist only after you've done all your homework, read this book and others, talked with adopters and adoptees, and realistically considered your choices. The more you know about the adoption process, the more your criteria are likely to change.

However, your list should include the things you are strongly committed to and those that you are willing to compromise.

Your form should leave room for information from each organization you contact. Be prepared to obtain answers for every question from each agency you consider. Always include your contact's name, phone number and dates of contact.

As you approach agencies and organizations, measure each one against your two checklists. Apply only to those that meet most of your key criteria and that tally well against our checklist of critical questions. If no agent or organization measures up, you may need to re-evaluate your criteria.

To fill out your checklists, first read all of the agency materials and take as much information from them as possible. You generally can rely on written information. Verbal input is less reliable. Only when you have absorbed the written materials should you follow up with the contact whose name you were given in response to your initial query. Your follow-up may be by phone or in person.

If possible, conduct your interview in person at the agency. When you are face-to-face, you are more likely to get comprehensive answers. In addition, you are underlining your sincerity and commitment and, perhaps, making friends with someone who can help you to adopt. Never underestimate positive contact with agency employees. Any small advantage can make the difference.

You also gain considerable insight into an organization when you make a personal visit. If their offices are shabby and chaotic, if there is little consideration for your time and needs, perhaps that is the way they run their adoption business as well. On the other hand, if the staff is well informed and helpful, you can be more confident.

This is not the time to be shy and self-effacing. Do not simply accept, because you don't want to offend anyone, whatever information the counselor may dole out. Of course, you are not there to confront. You are, however, there to get answers. So persist.

On the other hand, do not expect great amounts of anyone's time. Understaffing is a byword of the adoption business. Gather as much information as you can. Then make an appointment to get the rest of it by phone or set up another meeting.

If the information you seek is unavailable, note that on your checklist as well. If you find the agency too busy or unwilling to respond to your questions, seek out other sources who can fill in the blanks. State licensing bureaus can provide costs, timing and track records of various agencies. Other agency clients, both adoptive parents and birth parents, also can help, as can organizations such as Resolve, a self-help infertility group that has chapters around the country. If you are adopting out of state, contact the office of the Interstate Compact Administrator (see Chapter Six), which oversees all interstate adoptions. To find out whether any complaints have been registered against the agency, check with the state attorney general's office, the state agency that regulates adoptions, the court that oversees adoptions, and the Better Business Bureau.

Don't rule out an agency just because it doesn't answer all of your questions up front. Remember the glut of queries it must field. Keep in mind its record for successful placements and evaluate other key criteria before crossing it off your list. At this stage, you should pursue every reasonable option. Only after this initial information-gathering stage should you begin culling your choices.

As you ask your questions, compare the answers with

your personal criteria, the first checklist you developed. At any point during the questioning, you may determine an agency is not for you. Obviously, at that stage, there is no point in continuing with your interview.

THE RIGHT QUESTIONS—A CHECKLIST

• *Do you deal with people like us?*

For instance, geography may be a block. Some agencies do not work with clients who live beyond certain geographic boundaries.

• *Are there any criteria that would disqualify us?*

For example, if you are dealing with a fundamentalist Christian agency and you are of a different faith, you may not qualify.

• *Who is your client base?*

What kinds of people are you placing babies with? What are their common denominators?

• *How long have you been in business?*

If you are new in business, what qualifies you to conduct adoptions?

Perhaps an attorney or doctor doing adoptions has opened an agency. Fine. He or she is likely to have knowledge and sources. But if the people at the agency have minimal experience, they are less likely to have access to adoptable babies.

- *Are you licensed? By whom?*

An agency should be licensed by the appropriate state authority; a lawyer, by his state bar association. Some states require all adoption-placement organizations to be licensed. With this question, you can validate the organization as well as identify a reference.

- *What is the number of placements you do?*

Last year? The year before that? What is the trend in the number of your successful placements? Is it declining, increasing, or staying about the same?

There is no number too low, if everyone on the list receives a baby of his or her choice within two or three years or a reasonable period of time. However, if an agency only takes twenty couples a year, they may not be aggressively pursuing adoptions. If only a few adoptions are completed each year—say, ten or so—your choice of adoptable children will be sharply limited. There just will not be many different children to choose from.

Even if an agency is handling thirty adoptions a year, that only means two or three placements a month—not very many. Once you reach sixty placements annually, you're dealing with a fair-size agency likely to have significant experience.

- *What kinds of placements have you been making?*

Many agencies don't like to answer this question. They may tell you they made sixty placements last year, but, unless you probe, you may not learn the ages, the physical or mental condition, or the ethnic background of the children.

If the answer is vague, it may mean the agency does mostly minority, older, and special-needs adoptions. Follow up with other sources until you have a satisfactory answer. You'd also better know the expectations of the other parents on the agency's waiting list.

You may decide you want to adopt a hard-to-place child. But make that decision for the right reasons.

• *How long is the wait? Has it changed in the past five or ten years? How?*

Look at the trends. If the agency won't give out this information, you should wonder why. If, however, the wait is two years or less, you can be reasonably assured that there won't be major changes in the agency or in the availability of adoptable babies.

If the agency is vague about timing, that's another red flag. Or if it gives exceedingly broad parameters, like one to five years, follow up. Talk to other couples, both to those who have dropped out and to those who have been successful.

No state allows an agency or lawyer to be paid a fee for finding a baby. That's considered buying and selling babies. It is illegal to say, "If you sign with us, we guarantee we will place a child with you within a specific time after we receive your deposit."

The best you are going to get is, "We believe you will adopt within a certain time period." Most agencies set their own time estimates. One agency aims at placement within one year but tells their couples to expect a child between nine and sixteen months after entering their program.

• *How many couples are on your list? How many do you accept?*

Say the answer is three hundred. The agency told you it did thirty placements last year, and the wait is three years. Either it has an extraordinarily high dropout rate or something is wrong with the figures.

Make sure the size of the agency list corresponds reasonably to the wait and to the number of available babies. If the agency accepts a markedly disproportionate number of applicants compared with the number of placements, beware.

• *What is your dropout rate?*

There are many legitimate reasons someone drops off an agency's waiting list: pregnancy, success on another list, deciding against adoption for some reason.

These are the critical statistics, the numbers that reveal the truth few agencies are eager to disclose. If you are serious about adopting, consider no agency without applying the following formula.

The NUMBER OF WAITING COUPLES (in your category) minus the NUMBER OF WAITING COUPLES WHO ANNUALLY DROP OUT (in your category) divided by the NUMBER OF ANNUAL PLACEMENTS (in your category) equals the WAITING TIME TO ADOPT in years. (The definition of "in your category" would be a reflection of the number of couples waiting to adopt a child similar to one you are waiting for. For example, you are waiting to adopt a healthy newborn Hispanic infant. How many couples are waiting for the same type of child?)

W − D divided by P = T

If: Waiting couples = 100
Dropouts = 30
Placements = 35

Then: $\frac{100 - 30}{35} = 2$ years

If the number of other waiting couples, less the dropouts, far exceeds the number of placements, then your wait could be indefinite. This formula may need some adjustment if the agency, for example, has shown a yearly increase in placements, and the agency has added couples based on the projected increases.

• *How much do you charge and how is it paid?*

What are the actual costs? Are there any hidden costs? What could we conceivably be asked to pay for that you haven't mentioned?

What happens, for instance, if there are serious legal or medical problems? What if a Caesarean section is required? Who is going to pay for it? What if the birth mother changes her mind? Who pays then?

Most agencies and independents will give you a standard fee schedule. They will list what's covered and when payments are due. Sometimes, there is a sliding fee scale, depending on your income or the type of child you adopt.

You may have decided you want only one child, a healthy newborn, and you will do whatever it takes to succeed, including mortgaging your house to raise the money. Just make sure you have the correct figures. And don't forget that adoption costs are only the beginning.

Often state or federal programs can help with the costs incurred in an adoption. Many of the non-profit agencies' adoptions are subsidized. Most states will help with special-needs adoptions. The question is whether you qualify.

In any case, don't just pay an agency $20,000 in hopes that the required consent forms come through six months later. Be sure to find out whether you are liable for expenses if the adoption falls through.

Most licensed non-profit and for-profit agencies charge a flat fee for a successful adoption and average in the costs for birth mothers who do not place. This means that the successful adopters subsidize unsuccessful ones. When adopting through an agency, it is unlikely you would be required to pay for a birth mother who decides to keep her baby.

With independents, it's a different story. Whether or not an adoption is completed, you may well be required to pay some or all of the costs involved. In a private placement, you could be expected to pay not only medical bills but also legal and counseling fees for time spent and services rendered. Costs for private adoptions vary widely and can greatly exceed those for agency placements, especially in cases in which medical bills are high or several birth parents are involved before a couple has a successful adoption. (See the section on Understanding Fees in an Adoption at the back of this book.)

In most adoptions, there is some protection against extreme overcharging. A licensed adoption agency has its budget approved by the state. Independent adoptions are generally approved by the court on a dollar-for-dollar basis.

In any event, find out precisely what is covered by your insurance and at what point in the adoption proceedings your insurance company picks up an adoptive child under your dependent coverage. Also determine exactly what the agency fees do and do not cover. Insist on having all financial arrangements in writing, and do not make any payments until you are reasonably confident of the agency's reputation.

- *How do we get off the agency list?*

Will any fees be forfeited? What if we don't feel we can afford the costs of a particular adoption?

- *What if the child assigned to us does not work out?*

What if we don't want the child chosen for us? Or what if the birth mother chooses to keep her baby?

Will we be removed from the list, or dropped to the bottom? Or will we keep our place and be in line for the next appropriate baby?

It may be you will be asked to wait for the right

reasons. Often you can't just turn around and stand in line for the next baby who comes along. You may need additional counseling; you may need time.

• *What requirements do you have of participants in your program?*

Are participants required to attend meetings, pay certain fees, and fund agency activities? Will you be removed from the waiting list if you sign up with any other agencies?

Must a parent be home for a certain period of time with the baby? Are there additional requirements beyond the traditional home study? Are you expected to provide transportation, housing, or maternity clothes to birth mothers?

• *How do you communicate with those waiting on your list?*

What kind of a timetable should you expect? What happens when? How should we communicate with the agency?

• *Do you require and/or offer counseling?*

What does it include? What are the credentials of the person who conducts it? Is it group or individual counseling? What is the length of the program?

• *What do you require of birth parents?*

What programs, if any, do you provide for the birth mother? How do you deal with the birth father, if at all? What criteria do you have for your birth parents? Do you accept all birth mothers? Are you equipped to deal with any situation, such as drug abuse, older children, retardation, minorities?

If an agency works with every birth parent who seeks its help, it is not necessarily a negative. But you need to know this because it means the agency will be trying hard to place special-needs children.

• *How do you make a match?*

What say, if any, do the birth parents have in choosing the parents of their baby? Do we, as the adoptive parents, have any part in the matchmaking?

• *How much information do you have about the birth parents?*

Most agencies have a standard form on which they gather birth-parent information. Ask to see a sample so you will know what type of information you will be receiving. Find out whether you will be able to obtain further background if it becomes necessary. For instance, what if a medical problem surfaces in several years? Will you be able to get in touch with the birth parents or their doctor to ask specific questions, either directly or using the agency as an intermediary?

• *What is your policy toward open adoption?*

Agency policy can range from provision of minimal, non-identifying information to full disclosure and an ongoing, face-to-face relationship between adoptive and birth parents.

• *Do you condone searches for birth parents by your adoptees?*

What role, if any, do you play? What information do you keep on file?

• *May we have a reference list of adopting parents?*

Most agencies will be able to direct you to parents who have adopted through their programs. Adoptive couples are almost always eager to share their experiences. Of course, references will be those who were successful in adopting and are happy with the agency. Also, keep in mind that adoptive parents tend to be almost naively blissful once they have their baby at home. Nevertheless, there is a great deal to be learned from these references.

Because of the adoptive parents' right to confidentiality, an organization may not reveal information about them without their permission. Therefore, a list of parents and their addresses or telephone numbers may not be available. However, information may be available with the state licensing department, the Better Business Bureau, or in the case of an attorney, with the state bar.

Closed, Open, and Cooperative Adoptions

Although closed adoptions used to be the norm, the trend today is toward openness. Here's a look at the entire spectrum.

Closed Adoption

In a closed adoption, the privacy of everyone involved is paramount. Various amounts of non-identifying information (see Chapter Seven) are exchanged, usually including basic medical and social backgrounds. Closed adoptions began only about forty years ago in order to protect the birth mother and the child from stigma.

In the past, whatever information was available often was passed along verbally when a couple came to pick up their baby. The adoptive parents, distracted by their newborn, rarely concentrated on what they were told. So, years later, when the information became important, the parents couldn't remember any details.

Today, in a closed adoption, information almost always is shared in writing. Whenever you learn something new, no matter how important the information and how sure you are about remembering, take notes.

Open Adoption

Open adoption includes the exchange of identifying information. It runs along a continuum, from virtually no contact to extensive contact and involvement, so-called cooperative adoption. Most open adoptions involve initial contact around the time of placement and lessened contact as the years pass.

In an open adoption, the adoptee may or may not be in direct contact with his birth parents. Open adoption can mean a single meeting of the adoptive and the birth parents on neutral grounds without an exchange of names or addresses, or it may involve a deep friendship in which the parents and child regularly visit one another's homes. Those who have never adopted or who have not had much prior exposure to adoption issues usually opt for an adoption at the conservative end of the spectrum.

The birth mother is usually the one asking for an open adoption. She wants as much information as possible before she decides whether to place her baby. She also needs the reassurance that knowing provides.

Communication

Until recently, there was no communication whatsoever other than the third-party exchange of basic information. People simply would not adopt or place their baby for adoption if they felt there was even the remotest possibility of exposure.

Now, adoptive parents often promise to forward pictures and updates during the child's first year and often longer. However, nothing can force them to do so. Remember, there are no legal obligations between adoptive and birth parents that would affect the finality of the adoption process. You should realize, though, that birth parents treasure these communications. For example, one birth mother said that just seeing the smile of her baby in a picture proved to her that she made the right decision.

The following three letters appeared in "Dear Abby" columns. Consider this birth mother's feelings:

> Ten years ago, I gave birth to a daughter out of wedlock. Even though I subsequently married and have been blessed with two more daughters to love and raise,

> Mother's Day is the hardest day in the year for me. Not only was I unable to keep my firstborn, I know nothing about what kind of person she is; indeed, I don't even know if she is alive.

The writer goes on to ask that the adoptive parents, once a year, write to the adoption agency and provide updated information about the child's development, interests, activities and a little about their family life if they are willing.

In another example:

> Thirteen years ago, I gave up a baby girl. . . . Last year, I received a beautiful letter from the woman who adopted my daughter when she was five days old. She not only told me a great deal about my child's personality and character and interests, she enclosed some pictures of her. (I had to pinch myself to make sure I wasn't dreaming!) I don't know this woman's name or where she lives, and I will not try to locate her. Abby, never in my life did I expect to receive a gift so precious!

And this is from an adoptive mother:

> In the beginning, I spent hours wondering about *you,* her birth mother, the young woman who had the courage—and the love—to give away her child. By now I hope you've had other children to cherish. . . . Dear, dear friend, you gave her birth, but we tried to give her life—as abundantly as we were able.
>
> You would be so proud of her. For 25 years, I have

wanted to thank you for our daughter. She was, and is, the sunshine of our lives. . . . Why am I writing to tell you this now? You and I are going to be grandmothers. . . . I only pray that God has blessed your life as richly as ours has been blessed by Jean.

(Letters taken from the Dear Abby Column by Abigail Van Buren, © 1983 Universal Press Syndicate.)

It's a common misconception that providing information or sending pictures of a healthy, happy child will make the birth parents want their child back. Nothing could be further from the truth. Such information reaffirms their decision. It helps them to know they did the right thing.

In one open adoption, the birth mother, Karen, regularly obtains pictures of her baby, and her parents like to show them to friends. Others who know Karen sometimes wonder why she tortures herself this way, thinking she should put the baby out of her mind and get on with her life.

Karen needs to know how her baby is doing for her own peace of mind. She says she could never have agreed to a closed adoption.

"Every time I read about a child being kidnapped I would imagine it as mine. I would wonder where she was, what she was doing and what she looked like. Does her hair curl like mine and do her teeth need straightening?"

As Karen's mother says, "There are now three other people in Karen's life who are very special to her, her 'other family.' What will she [the baby] think of all this when she is old enough to understand? I feel that the love that flows from all of us and surrounds this tiny baby girl can't do anything but enhance her life."

Frequently, the birth mother writes her child a letter explaining the reasons she placed him for adoption. This type of letter is usually emotional and tells of the struggle to decide what is best for the child and why adoption was chosen, reaffirming the birth mother's love.

Some adoptive parents opt for agency-arranged telephone conversations with the birth parents. It gives them an opportunity to directly exchange information and ask questions while maintaining confidentiality.

One birth mother, on learning that her child was adopted by a family with several other children, was afraid that her child would not be an important family member. The child's adoptive mother got on the phone and told the birth mother how they loved her daughter and what she meant to them and how she was raising her children. Her call reassured the birth mother.

Face-to-Face Meetings

Because increasing numbers of birth parents help choose the parents for their children, more are asking to meet them. These meetings give the birth parent an opportunity to assess the adoptive parents. At the same time, the adoptive parents have an opportunity to learn firsthand about the birth mother.

In such meetings you might expect to discuss family

issues—how many other children you want to have, parenting concerns, hopes for the child. What kind of life will the child have? What are your hobbies? When and where do you go on vacation? Where do you live? What's your neighborhood like? Do you have pets? Do you like music?

Usually these meetings occur only after both parties have had a chance to evaluate each other's background information. At Southwest Adoption, Adoptions of New England, and Adoption Center of Washington, we recommend having a professional either set up the meeting and establish guidelines and/or be present to facilitate.

Here are some things to consider as you set up a meeting.

- Are you going to exchange names and addresses?
- Do you call each other by first names only?
- How long will the meeting last? (They can range anywhere from fifteen minutes to six hours, depending on your interest and agenda.)
- Where will you meet?
- Will you have your intermediary there? Who else will be there?
- What is the purpose of the meeting? Is the birth mother going to interview ten couples and then pick one? Or is this possibly her only meeting? Are you meeting more than one birth mother?
- Will the birth mother have any requirements of you?

- Are there subjects that are off-limits?
- Are there boundaries on the information exchanged?
- Has the birth mother been informed of, and agreed to, the ground rules?
- Do you have a list of topics and questions you want to discuss? (You should.)

Meeting after Placement

If you meet after placement, you forgo the worry of whether your birth mother actually will place her child with you. But both you and the birth mother can glean information you will treasure for a lifetime, details that cannot be transmitted on paper or thirdhand. The birth mother will want to know about her baby. How did you feel when you first saw your child? What is your time together like when you are with the child? If you have pictures, all the better. In some cases, the child is there, too.

Some parents worry that, in a cooperative type of open adoption, their child will have divided loyalties and be confused about who his parents really are. Or they think that contact with birth parents will have a negative influence on the child. Perhaps the child will develop a poor self-image if a birth parent is an alcoholic or a criminal. Sometimes, this fear is groundless. Other times, it is fully justified. Use your judgment about open adoption. Make your decision based on what you know about the birth parents. There are many advantages to an open adoption—but there can be disadvantages as well.

A birth parent may want to interfere in the way his or her child is being raised. In one case, a thirteen-year-old girl's adoptive parents were in their early fifties. The thirty-six-year-old birth father wanted to become involved in her life and provide a buffer against what he perceived as out-of-date parents.

What if the birth mother is having problems and has nowhere to turn? Are you obligated to help her? Will that get in the way of your parenting? What if she comes to you and says, "Look. You have a wonderful life. I gave you my baby. And I'm miserable. You owe me a better life." Explain your position, through a lawyer, if necessary. And never negotiate.

As for the issue of a birth parent coming back to take her baby away, it is virtually unfounded. In almost all cases, the decision has been made. The birth mother wants to move ahead with her life, without the baby. Remembering is not the same as reconsidering. She believes she did the right thing. She gave her baby the gift of a better life.

Cooperative Adoption

Sharon Kaplan, a cooperative-adoption counselor, defines "cooperative adoption" as "the child's access to both families, to both sets of parents, with progressive participation in the decisions that will affect his or her life."

According to proponents of cooperative adoption, it does not mean that the birth parents will be parenting;

it means that the child will not lose his rightful heritage. Most birth parents are interested in receiving pictures and letter updates regularly. A few ask for visitation rights once or twice a year.

The following conditions usually exist in a cooperative adoption:

- Birth parents choose the adoptive family.
- Birth and adoptive parents know each other's identity, location and biographical information, and both sides agree who will pay the adoption-related expenditures. They exchange ongoing medical data as well as hopes and dreams.
- Adoptive parents can see the birth family during pregnancy and/or the hospital stay and be present at birth.
- Names are added to, rather than changed, on the birth certificate, which is usually not sealed.
- The baby is usually placed directly in the adoptive home without foster care.
- Adoptive and birth parents and the adoptee can see all files and records.
- Families have ongoing, direct communications in person, by phone, or through letters and/or photos.
- The adoptee can know the birth family and be a progressive participant in the decisions and relationship surrounding the adoption.

One of the issues that comes up in cooperative adoption is the baby's name. Of course, the adoptive parents have the right to name their child, but often the adoptive and birth parents will do it together. Sometimes, birth parents will give the baby his middle name.

Many cooperative-adoption specialists require both client families to keep a day-to-day journal as soon as the process begins, so the child will have his or her adoption history later on in life. The doctor may be asked to write up a summary of the delivery as well. Each family also maintains a birthbook and scrapbook with all of the adoption information and mementos.

Some birth parents say the communication involved is too painful—that seeing even pictures hurts too much—so all communication is saved until they are ready.

In cooperative adoption, birth parents are not co-parents, and adoptive parents are warned to set limits. There are occasional abuses. For example, one adoptive couple gave a birth father $200 for a plane ticket. The couple was urged by their adoption counselor not to do it again.

In another situation, a birth mother's mother-in-law called the adoptive parents to tell them her daughter-in-law was going to jail because she owed $4,000 in past traffic tickets. The parents were reminded by their caseworker, "You are adopting her baby, not her."

Cooperative-adoption specialists encourage their clients to go through as many as ten interviews with birth mothers before making a decision and they warn of the rare birth mother who is interviewing scores of prospective parents. And adoptive couples are reminded, "If you don't care for the birth parents, don't take their baby."

Some adoptive couples worry that the child will be confused about his birth parents. For the child, the relationship with the birth parents can be like having another friend, another relative. The birth parent doesn't come into the child's house as if it were home.

Although at the far end of the open-adoption continuum, cooperative adoption can be as varied as the continuum itself. In some cases, after initial contact, there is nothing further—ever. In other cases, close friendship evolves. It depends on how much the parents have in common and how much they like one another.

Obviously, you have to have a strong level of maturity to carry through effectively with a cooperative adoption. For this reason, most couples who are involved with a cooperative adoption are over thirty years old.

THE RIGHT QUESTIONS TO ASK AUTHORITIES ABOUT AN AGENCY

If you have completed your agency checklist and it compares favorably with your personal checklist—and if you feel good about the organization on all counts—then proceed to the final information-gathering stages.

Go to the courts handling adoptions, the juvenile

authority, and the state licensing office and ask the following:

- *Do you handle many adoptions from this agency?*
- *Have there been any complaints against it?*
- *Are adoptions often continued or delayed? Do the agency's adoptions sail through the system efficiently every time? Are there any problems?*

If there have been legal problems, what do they involve? Has the agency been trying to do too much? Are the birth mothers going without appropriate counseling and changing their minds at the last minute? Does the agency place babies in foster care prior to adoption when it isn't absolutely necessary? Does the lawyer or agency have a substantial adoption practice with few court problems? Or are there too many complaints?

OK. Assume several of your targeted agencies and/or independents get enthusiastic approval from the regulating and legal authorities. And they have high scores on your checklist. Now move on to your reference list, particularly to parents who have adopted through the agency, with the following questions:

QUESTIONS TO ASK REFERENCES

- *What do you think of the agency's program?*
- *What kind of baby did you adopt?*

Is that what you were looking for when you went on the agency's list? Did you change your mind along the way? Did the agency offer you any other children before you chose the child you finally adopted?

This line of questioning helps you in two areas. One, you can see whether an agency exerts any pressure on prospective parents to adopt hard-to-place children. And two, you can determine whether the agency is placing the type of children adoptive parents request when they enter the program.

• *What were you told when you went on the list?*

What representations were made? Did the agency live up to them? Were the people you dealt with honest and forthcoming?

• *How long did you wait for your child?*

Does that correspond with what you were told?

• *Was the cost approximately what you were told it would be?*

Were there any hidden costs or any surprises relating to your expenses or fees?

• *Did the rules change after you were in the process?*

How? Why? Have there been any changes in the administration of the agency?

• *How were the agency employees to deal with?*

Is there anyone we should ask to work with? Is there anyone we should avoid?

• *What requirements did the agency have of you?*
Did they change after you were on its list? Did you know about them ahead of time?

• *How did you become a client?*

• *How do you feel coming out of the program?*

• *How should we communicate with the agency?*
Do we need to call regularly?

• *How do we know if the agency feels we are good prospective parents?*
What is to prevent it from moving us down the list and making us wait longer?

• *Is there anything we should be aware of that could go wrong? What should we be careful of?*

• *Does the agency have ongoing support groups? How did they help you, if they did?*

• *Is there a downside?*
Was there ever a time while you were waiting that you felt your adoption was in jeopardy? Why? (After you ask these questions, outline the terms you discussed with the agency. Then ask the references, Is this what they told you? Did they live up to those promises?)

• *Would you use the agency again?*

• *Do you know others we should talk to?*
Are there people with experiences different than yours, people who may have had problems whom we

could contact? Do you know anyone who went off the agency's list? (These are important questions, for you may discover someone who has had a negative experience with the agency. Obviously, the people referred directly by the agency can be expected to be enthusiastic. Possibly they are major contributors to the agency or lay preachers for the affiliated religious organization. You may hear a different story from others not directly referred by the agency.)

- *What else should we know?*

You may be surprised by the unexpected response this simple question can evoke. This is where a happy adoptive couple may admit they waited longer or paid more than anticipated in their adoption.

When you have completed this information-gathering stage, draw up a short list of those agencies you would feel comfortable working with. Do not be too restrictive until you are confident that your personal checklist will be fulfilled by a targeted agency. Until you are selected and firmly on an agency list, keep at least three agencies on your short list.

CHAPTER FOUR

Making the Cut: How an Agency Chooses You

You've completed your initial homework. You've learned a lot, probably more than you expected. You now have a short list of three or more agencies, organizations, lawyers, or approaches you believe can best help you adopt.

Your goal now is to take the steps that will fix the odds in your favor, to be accepted onto the adoption lists of your target organizations.

Now is the time to review your situation objectively. How do you fit with the agencies you have targeted? Do they work with people who are pretty much like you? Are you insisting on a perfect newborn from an elite agency that requires its adoptive parents to be ten years younger and a different religion than you?

Don't waste your time. Make sure your source or

sources can produce for you. Be realistic. Narrow your choices to as many agencies as you think you can comfortably deal with. It may be one. It may be more. Read this book, and others, before making your final decision, so you understand what is involved as you move ahead.

If you take a hard look at your situation and realize that the sources on top of your list will never accept you, regroup, rethink, and reapply the first steps to other possibilities.

Our goal in this book is to explore all possibilities. Thus, we detail much that can go wrong, so there will be no surprises. Remember that your reasons for going through the process is the happy ending. As you work through it, keep that in mind.

Once you are confident of your sources, be prepared to endure a long, often frustrating, process of qualification. For some, it is remarkably smooth. For most, it is a stressful, demanding time. If you do your homework, though, you can make your wait easier.

The qualification process differs from state to state and agency to agency. But some state requirements, such as the home study (see later in this chapter), are universal. And all adoptions involve a seemingly endless stream of forms, which often are repetitive and occasionally intrusive.

Don't think you can bypass the paperwork by working with a private or non-traditional adoption source. All states require comprehensive background information in order to protect a child's welfare.

You probably will encounter the following *Steps to*

Adoption in some form, not necessarily in the order listed, depending on your agency's way of doing business and on the laws in the state where you and your child will live.

APPLICATION

Most agencies have rules and guidelines you must follow. In some cases, before you fill out the written application and submit a fee, you will be pre-qualified over the telephone, which means you are found acceptable under the agency's criteria for age, mental state, and/or religion. After being pre-qualified, you may attend a group briefing, where you will hear about the adoption program. Many agencies give you information only on a need-to-know basis, and this can be frustrating because your questions may go unanswered.

Usually, though, the written application comes first. Most agencies will charge you a fee to review your application. The fee, together with the volume of required paperwork, deters you from sending applications out indiscriminately and helps underline your commitment.

Complete an application only if you mean it.

How many applications will you complete? This depends on your chances with each source, your willingness to deal with repetitive paperwork, and the agencies' requirements.

Perhaps you will complete only one application, confident you will be accepted on that agency's list. Maybe you will send in ten applications, and out of those, two acceptances will come back. If you have done a thorough investigation and come up with two or three sources you feel comfortable with, that is plenty.

You may be surprised by how much work must be done up front. Because agencies want to discourage people from shopping, they often require a great deal of information at this initial stage. They want to know that you are going to invest the effort required to complete the process. At this point, it is entirely possible you will realize that the effort simply is not worthwhile for you. Fine. This is the time to make that decision.

You probably will be asked to supply the following in your first formal application:

- Identifying information: name, age, address, race, sex.
- Religion.
- Occupation.
- Income level.
- Family situation.
- Medical records and results of a current, thorough physical examination. Perhaps a certificate from your doctor affirming your infertility, if applicable.
- Income-tax records.
- Education.

- Details of any problems such as bankruptcy, mental or physical illness, drug or alcohol addiction, criminal record.
- Color pictures of yourself and your home. Maybe pictures of the room where your child would sleep. Pictures of your pets, you and your hobbies, your other children, if you have any.
- Fingerprints.
- Your autobiography. (If a couple, one for each of you.) This should include the reasons you want to adopt; your lifestyle, interests; your childhood, describing significant events and favorite childhood activities; relationship with parents; information about your education, past marriages, your current marriage, family members, a description of how you would parent, your hopes and dreams for your new child.
- The type of child you want to adopt.

At some point in your adoption process, information about nearly all of these will be required, perhaps not in your initial application, but almost certainly before acceptance onto an agency list, particularly if the agency has a pre-acceptance initial interview with you. Depending on an agency's policy, when the time comes, some of the above may be shared with prospective birth parents.

Once you have decided to apply, be thorough. Do everything that is asked of you. Fill out the forms completely. If you are asked for pictures, submit them. If the agency wants records, send them. If you don't do what is asked, either you will lose time (because the forms will be sent back to you for completion), or more probably, you will simply be ignored and turned down.

Prospective adoptive parents are understandably nervous about the interrogation to which they are subjected. Many are offended as well.

"So what if I was divorced seven years ago?"

"What right do you have to judge my religion, my morals, my sex life?"

But if you want to adopt a healthy newborn, by now you know that demand overwhelms supply and noncompliance with agency requirements can mean no acceptance into the program. And you know that a baby's welfare is the priority in the adoption triangle. Before placing their baby, birth parents are typically going to do everything they can to ensure he or she will have the best possible life. That usually translates into a loving, stable home with two parents and an extended family and support system. It may come down to details such as having a dog, living in the country, or having red hair.

So, how do you deal with all these questions? Most important, always be honest. You don't want to be caught in a lie. Then everything else is suspect. Remember, the information you give can—and almost always will be—checked out.

On the other hand, don't go overboard. The people reviewing your application know you're trying to present your best side. If you describe every mistake you've ever made, they'll wonder why.

Think about the purpose of these forms. Approach

them as you would any job application. You are applying for the position of parent. The agencies want to see what you can offer a baby.

If you present yourself as totally problem-free, either you won't be believed, or you'll be perceived as incapable of dealing with unforeseen crises. If you have never had to deal with a problem or overcome a challenge, how could you possibly cope with a baby?

There is a gray area here, and only you can judge how to proceed. What about problems that you feel relatively sure will disqualify you? For example, if you had a drinking problem, and you solved it on your own, do you put this in writing?

Make a distinction between what you put on paper and what you talk about later in interviews with a social worker. Only you can know how far you can go with your caseworker. In an interview, you have an opportunity to put things in context, to explain yourself.

Think, too, about the *pictures* you include, unless you subconsciously want to be rejected. One couple sent a picture of themselves with the giggling wife seated on her husband's lap, highball glasses in hand. Surely not the image to present to an unknown social worker looking at hundreds of other applicants.

What about *confidentiality*? Will your income-tax forms be passed around? Legally, an agency provides full confidentiality. But you can't guarantee that a clerk processing your papers won't pass some information along. If you have concerns, it is certainly appropriate to ask for assurances from anyone you are working with in the course of trying to adopt.

To some people, privacy is all-important. They may choose to adopt through an attorney or other private source because they feel there are fewer people aware of their personal affairs in that setting.

RESPONSE TO YOUR APPLICATION

Most licensed agencies will respond to your application within a specified time. There have been so many cases of agencies holding onto applications indefinitely (while applicants hold their breaths or, worse, incorrectly believe they have been accepted), that many states have written response times into law.

For example, in Arizona, licensed agencies are required to respond to an applicant within ninety days. This prevents thousands of applications from sitting on a desk collecting dust. And it forestalls someone from assuming, "They've been reviewing me for six months. They must like me."

Be sure to understand the policies of the source to whom you are applying as well as the laws of the states in which you apply. You do not want to waste time waiting for application responses and thereby forfeit an opportunity to be placed on a different list.

Don't be afraid to clarify this issue or any other unresolved question about an agency from Chapter Three.

If you have no response within the specified period, call and ask. Every agency has an individual responsible for application review who can respond to your inquiry.

If you are turned down without an explanation, do not hesitate to find out why. And if you prefer, ask for the reason in writing.

For instance, there may be an upper age limit. If you are forty-nine, you are going to have to be more flexible about the type of child you will accept and/or whose list you go on. If you are in a program where the birth parents select from parent profiles and they have a wide range of couples in their twenties and thirties to choose from, you may never be chosen. Again, be realistic, so you can maximize your position and consider alternate approaches.

There are always exceptions. Jimmy Durante, in his later years, was chosen in an open-adoption setting in California by a birth mother who felt that the advantages offered by a well-known comedian outweighed the disadvantage of his age. Likewise, something in your background may spark the interest of the agency or the birth parents who choose your adoption profile.

On the other hand, you may be turned down for reasons totally unrelated to your qualifications or personal profile. An agency may simply have closed its intake. Or it may not have any available babies. Don't be discouraged. Getting turned down is a normal part of the process. Be sure you understand the reason your application was denied and go on.

If you are rejected, *always* ask where else to look and whom you can talk to there. At this stage of your search, you must continue to explore all reasonable possibilities. And there are many.

ACCEPTANCE

You've been accepted—a cause for celebration. But remember not to lose sight of your goal. Pause here. Evaluate thoroughly. Whether you have one or more acceptances, consider carefully. Go back to our equation in Chapter Three and apply it again.

The NUMBER OF WAITING COUPLES (in your category) minus the NUMBER OF WAITING COUPLES WHO ANNUALLY DROP OUT (in your category) divided by the NUMBER OF ANNUAL PLACEMENTS (in your category) equals the WAITING TIME TO ADOPT in years.

If the agency passes the test of the formula, then, once again, think. Can you afford it? Even the unexpected, hidden costs?

What about the timing? Can you wait five years if a particular agency would need that much time to arrange a successful adoption? Go back through our checklist and re-evaluate. Then make your final choice.

You may decide to go on several lists. This is an independent call, hinging on your finances, the policy of the agencies, your adoptive profile, and your time.

There usually are two, perhaps more, levels of acceptance. The first acceptance means you have been added to the agency waiting list. At least one further but less risky acceptance level hinges on the home study.

At this point, if you decide to go onto an agency's waiting list, there may be an additional fee. Up-front fees vary widely and can run anywhere from $50 to $2,500. Be sure to ask the agency policy about refunding part or all of your fees if you decide to leave the agency. Public agencies are the exception; they usually don't charge at this stage. If they do, it's minimal.

The agency may request even more data and information from you to supplement your application. It may want you to flesh out your autobiography. It may want more records. Whatever is requested, if you want to be on their list, do it. And do it as quickly as you can. The clock doesn't start ticking until your materials are complete.

Working Exclusively with One Agency

Some agencies demand exclusivity. Others don't care. In any event, your files are confidential. Be aware, however, that you may forfeit up-front fees and be dropped from an agency's list if its staff learns you've broken an exclusivity agreement.

You should consider the paperwork required, the home study, and the duplication of your effort. If an agency does not require exclusivity, you may be able to use the same home study for more than one agency. If it does, you may need a second home study if you want to pursue a second agency.

ORIENTATION

An orientation process can fall anywhere in the first sequence of events. At orientation, you have an opportunity to ask questions and gather further information. Your target agency may not have answered all your questions up front. Now is the time to ask.

Here is an overview of what information you can expect to receive during the orientation process, regardless of where it comes in the sequence of events.

- How the agency works, its history, its goals.
- Who qualifies?
- What your responsibilities are.
- What the agency's responsibilities are.
- What you can expect in the program.
- The probable timetable.
- Information on temporary custody before adoption.
- List of reading materials, support groups.
- Legal ramifications and requirements.
- Social services, required and available.
- How the agency works with birth parents.
- What kind of contact you can expect to have with the agency.
- How open the adoption process is.
- When and how a match is made for you.
- Your payment schedule.

- Who you will be dealing with at the agency.
- Answers to your insurance coverage questions.
- General advice.

Again, remember: This may be one of few opportunities to ask key questions. Go prepared with a checklist (see Chapter Three). It is easy to forget one of your questions in your excitement. If the answers offered at the orientation are different from written or verbal information received from the agency or by means of your own investigation, then ask the agency to clarify these differences. Even though you may be singled out as a potential troublemaker in some agencies, it is better to get the answers now than to be disappointed later.

THE HOME STUDY

This step is mandatory. It is also notorious—sometimes justifiably, sometimes not. The home study is just that, a "study" of your home, your environment, your ability to parent. A social worker will conduct the study and decide whether he or she can recommend you as an adoptive parent. Almost all agencies have staff who are qualified to complete both the home study and a later supervisory report to the court, which is usually required after your baby is placed with you. If you are not working with an agency, you will be assigned a licensed social worker, typically from an agency or the state.

Almost inevitably, home studies are favorable. In fact, a home study can be a positive learning experience. There is enormous disparity here. A home study can consist of anything from a phone call to a group meeting to a series of up to six visits at your home. Usually, however, an office meeting and at least several home visits are involved.

Just as is the case with any personal evaluation, your study is a reflection of the person conducting it. Unfortunately, a home study can deteriorate into a personal intrusion. It all depends on your social worker, and there's not much you can do except comply as best you can. Remember that most social workers want to package happy families. The system is in your favor.

Usually, a home study takes from two to six months to complete, and it generally remains valid for twelve to twenty-four months. In most states, you can update your home study after the year has elapsed to carry through for up to two more years. An update is relatively simple to obtain.

A typical home study might include an office meeting and perhaps two or three visits to your home, including interviews with the two of you together, if you are a couple, and each of you individually. Each session may last one to four hours. The objective is to develop a realistic view of your lifestyle and your home.

Your agency will schedule the home-study appointments. If you and/or your spouse work, you'd probably like your meetings on weekends and in the evenings. Don't try it. Social workers keep traditional hours and need to schedule you during them. They save their overtime for the arrival of babies. So unless it is suggested otherwise, don't antagonize your counselor by trying to make yourself the exception.

You probably will be assigned times and dates by your agency, often with little or no input from you. In the counselor's view, these meetings are a priority, ahead of your business trip, your vacation, your family reunion.

At most agencies, you will jeopardize your very adoption by failing to comply with the schedule of visits. You may risk being dropped to the end of the waiting list. At the least, you risk offending the person who holds the future of your adoption in his or her hands.

What will you be asked? See the Sample Home Study in the back of this book; also see the rest of this chapter. Remember, by definition, a home study is an evaluation of your personal life. Your social worker may or may not be less affluent, less educated, less mature, and less experienced in life than you. The counselor probably has never adopted, may not be married, and may not have children.

A home study is a subjective, judgmental situation, and some people resent it. Remember that the agency is trying to find the best possible family for the baby entrusted to it. Put yourself in the position of the social worker. How would you place the baby? What would you do?

Another consideration: The more the agency knows about you, the better the match can be. For instance, if music is important to your family and the agency has a musical birth mother, then you are likely to be considered for the match. If you are a sportsman, perhaps the agency will match you with the baby of a man who lettered in football.

Some people enjoy the home study because it is a process of self-discovery. How often do you sit down and review your life? You may discuss your marriage or have the opportunity to get some help with your feelings about infertility. You may for the first time actively confront how a baby will change your life. Take advantage of your social worker's experience and knowledge.

Remember that your social worker is a professional and a unique resource on adoption. He or she probably knows as much about adoption as anyone else you will come in contact with (if not more), and can offer you resources, answers, feedback, and support.

You may find you actually like your social worker. (Although social workers are both male and female, the chances of having a female caseworker are substantially greater than having a male.) One couple spent the entire day with their counselor and then invited her to dinner; they have been friends ever since. And they have tapped into a splendid resource as well. Because you are sharing such an intimate part of yourself, you may develop a special bond, much like that of a pregnant woman and her obstetrician.

One couple learned that their social worker had died

of a heart attack. They postponed their adoption because they just couldn't imagine continuing the process with anyone else.

On the other hand, your social worker might be overly judgmental. One couple was given a negative report by a twenty-one-year-old unmarried social worker who was offended because their home-study visit frequently was interrupted by long-distance phone calls. She simply didn't understand how people so busy could make time for a baby. Or perhaps your social worker has been in the business for thirty years. She has become rigid and will hold you to an old-fashioned standard.

As you begin to work with your caseworker, assess that person carefully. Note biases, warmth, ability to compromise. Will your caseworker be your advocate or your judge? Use some judgment deciding how you will respond and interact with the caseworker. Get a feel for who you are dealing with and try to decide what she is looking for.

Before you begin talking about yourself, try to get some feedback. You might be honest and say, "I'm nervous about this. What can we expect?" The response alone may be infinitely revealing.

"I will ask the questions. We have certain criteria you must fit."

Or, "I'm here to learn about you. This is not supposed to be a threatening process."

Frankly, your first goal is to have the caseworker *like* you. If you are a relaxed couple and your social worker is strict and severe, think about how you will approach that person. You each have your own values. You probably will not be identical. But you can respect each other and develop a rapport. No matter what, you are going to be evaluated.

Do you need to score an A+? An emphatic no. Your social worker is not looking for perfection. In fact, as we've said, perfection is justification for suspicion. The question here is, *Are you physically, financially, emotionally, and morally fit to adopt?*

The golden rule: *Tell the truth.* Your answers are checked. If you are caught in a lie, it is almost impossible to be approved to adopt. If you tell the truth, your agency staff may be able to understand your problem and work with you. In most cases, you will recall, it is *your* agency's social worker who ultimately gives you the stamp of approval.

Read or listen to questions carefully. Generally, it is best to respond directly to the question that is asked, without offering additional information. If you have a choice and there is a gray area, explain a situation verbally, rather than committing something to writing. If you must put something in writing, attach an addendum explaining what happened and hope for an empathetic reader. In almost all situations, you can count on your explanation being read and considered.

Following is a list of the various topics included in a home study. You may be asked some of these questions prior to the home study when you register with an agency. But in one form or another, you will be asked to provide essentially the same information.

Reasons for Wanting to Adopt

In Chapter One, you were asked to do self-analysis to determine if adoption is the right way to have a family. Many of the questions you confronted are similar to ones asked during the home study. Of course, the difference is that the home study is prepared by an independent social worker.

Your social worker is looking for red flags here, such as: "My wife needs something to do," or, "Our parents are counting on a grandchild."

Some "acceptable" answers:

- I want to be a parent.
- I love to do things with children.
- Our life isn't complete.
- We want to share our love.
- We want to grow together with the next generation.

You shouldn't have to rehearse or guess the right answer; your response should be a natural one.

The Kind of Child You Want to Adopt

Don't tell the social worker what you think he or she wants to hear. Say only what you mean. You probably will be asked to qualify the following categories as ideal, acceptable, possible, or not acceptable.

- Newborn.
- Male.
- Female.
- Twins.
- Siblings.
- Caucasian.
- Black.
- Hispanic.
- Indian.
- Black/Caucasian.
- Hispanic/Caucasian.
- Asian/Caucasian.
- Other nationality.
- Unknown father.
- Child of rape.
- Child with correctable problem.
- Premature baby.
- Physical handicap.
- Mental handicap.
- Older child.
- Child with a family history of mental illness, incest, drugs/alcohol abuse, criminality, mental retardation.

As you go through this process, think about your own family history. You probably have relatives—maybe close ones—who have dealt with alcoholism, mental illness, cancer, asthma. Try to adopt normalcy, not perfection, as a standard.

Many first-time adoptive couples overreact to health histories. If a couple objects to a normal newborn with the average number of family medical problems in its genes, then adoption may never be the right solution for them.

Your Marital History

Do you have a satisfactory relationship? Is there room for anyone else? Will you want to continue to be together? Have you had many marital crises? Why are you still together? How do you view each other? How do you deal with differences in opinion? Give some examples. How do you communicate with each other?

Review the history of your relationship. How did you meet? What do you like about each other? Who makes the decisions? Did you live together before you married? (Be careful here if you are dealing with a traditional, religiously oriented agency.) Why did you marry? How has your relationship changed since the honeymoon? Have you ever been separated? (This is not necessarily a negative if you worked it out and your marriage is now stronger than before. It means you can deal with problems.)

Generally, if you have been together for one year or less, you will not have enough history. The social worker is looking for at least three or four years together. More progressive social workers will factor in the amount of time you lived together before you were married, but virtually no one will consider an unmarried couple.

Were you married before? What happened? Why? How is this marriage different? Perhaps you were extremely young and had little in common with your spouse. You are older, more mature, and more aware of the commitment it takes to have a successful marriage. Most agencies will accept that answer.

If you have been married three or more times, however, you will need to explain yourself thoroughly to satisfy your caseworker. Imagine the birth mother hearing that you have been divorced two or more times. Think about what you would say to make her believe this marriage is forever. Your social worker will consider the length of your prior marriages and your age at the time.

Essentially, the social worker wants to know that you have a solid, relatively normal relationship with a better-than-average chance of enduring through the minor years of your child.

Family Background

How do your family members feel about your marriage? What is your relationship with them (including in-laws) now? Are they close to you? How do they feel about your adopting? Perhaps they are totally opposed. Will that matter?

Is there anyone else in your support system? This

can be critical if your birth mother insists on an extended family.

You will be asked to discuss your family history. The social worker will want to know where you were born and how you were reared. How did your family get along? Did your parents have a happy marriage? Do you have brothers and sisters? What was the order of birth? Who else was important as you grew up—aunts and uncles, cousins?

How were you disciplined? Were you spanked? Maybe that was acceptable then but it will probably raise questions now. How will you discipline your child? What were your family values? As you grew up, what were your interests? What kinds of activities did you participate in? What was your education? What were your favorite and least favorite subjects? What were your interests in school?

Usually, there will be a correlation here between your upbringing and the one you plan for your child. Either you will want to offer the same kind of environment, or you will want to ensure that he or she has different and better opportunities.

If you've served in the military, discuss your service and how it affected you.

What are your hopes and dreams? What in your life would you like to change? Why?

Religious Activity

This can be important if an agency is looking for a particular religion. Or if the birth parents want their child raised in a specific religion.

You will almost always be asked to identify your religion and tell how important it is in your life. If you and your spouse are of different religions, you probably will discuss how you will work that out. How will you raise your child? How religious are you?

Some agencies will ask you to sign a statement of faith. You may be asked to rear your child in a certain way.

As always, don't lie. What if you say you go to church every week, and the pastor tells your caseworker he doesn't know you?

On the other hand, religion is a personal matter and most caseworkers will accept the statement that you have strong religious beliefs but you do not attend church every week.

Finances

This area of inquiry usually is more a question of how you manage your money, rather than how much you make. Essentially, your caseworker wants to know that you have more coming in than going out. He or she wants to be sure you can support your new child from diapers through braces and, generally, college.

You will be asked to verify your financial standing with bank records, tax returns, and other applicable documents. Do you have savings, any inheritances or trust funds? You may be asked how much you contribute to charity and to your church or synagogue each year.

Describe your job. If you are not employed, discuss your previous work. You probably will be asked to talk about your responsibilities, any special training or expertise you have, your career path, how you feel about your current situation, whether you are working or at home, what you like and don't like, and your goals.

You must be solvent. Job stability is important. If you have just been laid off or had an inexplicable succession of jobs, how will you support your new baby? If you both are working, will one of you quit work? If so, how will you manage?

What about your assets? Do you own your home or any property? What do you have to fall back on if necessary? You don't need to be landed gentry, but you do have to have a reasonably stable financial situation, including plans for an emergency.

If you have declared bankruptcy in the past, it doesn't mean automatic rejection. It does mean you need to explain it thoroughly. You may have a perfectly logical business reason. Or a medical emergency. On the other hand, if bankruptcy means a basic inability to deal with day-to-day problems, you're in trouble.

Lastly, what insurance do you have? Will it cover the birth mother's hospital delivery? When does your insurance kick in to cover your child? Your social worker also will want to know that you have other standard insurance coverage—life, home, property, automobile.

Understand that you are not required to be wealthy. You are expected to be stable. Some agencies may run a credit check.

Child-Care Plan

How will you care for your child on a day-to-day basis? Who will be responsible for what? An agency may require one parent to take time off—sometimes three or more years—to nurture a baby. If there will be any role reversals, how will that work out?

Your caseworker also will want to know that you have thought about schooling, parenting issues, and family interaction. What can you offer a child and what will you expect from him or her? Why will you be a good parent?

Will you need help because you both work or you have more than one child at home? Where will you find that help?

Medical/Health Issues

You will be asked to verify that you are physically and mentally healthy enough to rear a child. You must submit results of an up-to-date comprehensive physical examination and include a recent (within the last twelve months) chest X-ray and tuberculosis test.

If you are disabled, you will be asked to prove that your disability won't significantly affect your ability to parent. If you have other children, you will be asked to provide medical records for them as well.

The agency wants to ensure that you are likely to live for the natural course of your child's developmental years. Your caseworker or agency may react negatively to the following:

- Extreme obesity.
- Anorexia.
- Chronic, severe psychiatric problems.
- Severe medical problems.
- A physical handicap that could restrict parenting ability.

As always, there are gray areas. If you have a good prognosis and a good attitude, a disability may not prevent you from adopting.

But you also may remain on the agency's list for ten years without receiving a child. Competition means the children are likely to go to the most appealing families. If this is your situation, don't give up. Be realistic and pursue avenues that are most likely to be successful.

Existing Children in the Family

Your caseworker will want to know about your other children and how they are being or were reared. What is your relationship with them, and how will they feel about your adopting? Do they want to help with your new child? Will you give them some responsibilities for the new family member? If you are divorced, do you support your children? If they are older, are you in contact with them? (If you are not in contact, you will be expected to have a good reason.) How do they get along with your extended family?

Your Home

Here, your caseworker will explore your home, your neighborhood, your community resources, your lifestyle. You do not have to hide your liquor or dust the tops of your picture frames. Despite what you may have heard, this is not a white-glove inspection. However, if your house has obvious problems, such as filth, that could affect a child, questions will be raised.

Your home should be relatively clean and welcoming to a child. If you have white carpets and sofas, and crystal collections on all your glass tables, you probably will be asked how you will cope.

Your social worker will look for hazards. If you have a pool, is it fenced? Do you have any unusual or potentially dangerous pets? If you live on a busy street, is your yard fenced? If you live in an area that could pose any danger for your child, clarify what preventive arrangements you will make.

Where will your child sleep? Typically, the caseworker will describe your house, including the type of living arrangements planned for your child, in a report to the court.

Often adopting parents have pets. That's generally seen as a sign of potential parenting ability, especially if your dogs and cats are well cared for. You will need to consider how your animals will react to a new child.

You will be asked about schools and services in your neighborhood. What community resources are available for you and the child?

Your social worker also will want to know about your interests and hobbies. Are you involved in civic or church activities? Do you travel? Are you active in any sports or exercise? How do you spend your free time? How flexible are you? How will you deal with the restrictions a baby will impose on your lifestyle?

If you are so tightly programmed that there seems little room for giving, be careful. You must have space in your life for parenting.

Attitude Toward Adoption

Are you going to tell your child about this adoption? How? When? What kind of relationship would you like with the birth parents? Who do you believe are the *real* parents of an adopted child? Have you thought about how you might react if your child decides to find his or her birth parents later in life?

Do you know others who have adopted? Have you been through adoption education and counseling?

Have you read any adoption books or articles? These issues are critical to your social worker, who will hope for an enlightened attitude or, at the least, one based on thought and study.

Almost inevitably, the social worker will expect you to raise your child knowing about the adoption. He or she will want to know that you have a reasonable attitude about the birth parents, that you have done enough research to understand they are not a threat to you. If you would be willing to help your child search for the birth parents when he or she becomes an adult, so much the better.

References

The social worker conducting the home study is looking for character references—people who know you and can speak to the issue of adoption and you. You don't want your agency to get a letter from a reference saying, "I don't really know this couple very well." Your agency will presume that either you don't have any friends or at least don't know who your real friends are.

References can include both relatives and non-relatives. If you are active in your religion, your priest or rabbi would be a good choice. Try to include at least one person who knew you as you grew up and can speak positively about your family background. Try to include someone who has seen you interact with children and can comment from that perspective.

Typically, your references will be asked to make general statements about you as a person, as a parent. They will be asked about your lifestyle, specifically whether you have any bad habits that would affect your ability to parent, and how long they have known you. They will be asked questions such as, "Would you want your child taken care of by these people?"

One thing is certain. Your references will be checked, and checked carefully. Know ahead of time what your references will say about you. Do not take any chances. Call each potential reference, ask his OK to use his name, explain that a social worker will be calling or meeting with him, and go over his answers in detail. Someone may comment, "Sure, I'll be happy to be a reference," but that doesn't mean he'll provide the kind of positive, reassuring information that will impress a social worker to think favorably of your candidacy as an adoptive parent.

In one case, a reference told the social worker that the adopting couple frequently had a third sexual partner. In another case, a neighbor described a couple's late-night drinking bouts and loud fights.

In some cases, subconsciously, you may want help in *not* adopting. Or perhaps you simply don't realize what people will say. If you want to keep your adoption on track, do your homework with your references.

Red Flags

Couples are rarely turned down because of the home study. After all, your social worker is there to make adoptions happen. He or she is predisposed to like you. You are choosing to adopt and to love a child.

However, there can be derailments. Some causes for rejection were mentioned earlier in this chapter; others are listed below. In some cases, these, too, can be overcome:

- Missing child-support payments.
- Severe drug or alcohol abuse.
- Homosexuality.
- Commission to a mental hospital.
- Conviction of a felony or crime of moral turpitude.
- Severe medical handicap.

Again, the first rule is: *Never lie about your background.* If you do, your agency probably will find out and then it will be almost impossible to salvage your adoption. If the agency requires fingerprinting, then you have been run through an FBI check, or at least a statewide police check. What if you have an arrest record? Remember, all arrests—even for charges you may have been cleared of—will appear on your record.

If you have a serious problem, you have several options. You can tell your story up front and risk being cut from the agency's list before you have a chance to explain. This depends on your rapport with your social worker and your agency. Or you can answer questions literally and technically, not volunteering any additional information, at least initially in writing. If the agency finds out later, you may be able to explain yourself. Or the agency may, in fact, determine that you were lying by omission and cross you off their list.

Perhaps your best option, if you can manage it, is to describe your situation verbally to your social worker. You will have an opportunity to explain yourself fully and sympathetically. You have a better chance if your trouble involved a single incident, or if you have taken some sort of corrective action, or if the incident occurred many years ago.

For example, maybe you are a recovering alcoholic and have been participating in Alcoholics Anonymous for six years. Perhaps, after letting child-support payments slide, you have apologized and made payments with interest. But if you committed a crime just three months ago, you had better have a good explanation, together with documentation, showing you received counseling or took other appropriate action.

If the question in writing is very clear, answer it and try to explain. Attach an addendum, if necessary.

In general, problems in the past twelve months are virtually impossible to explain. Be prepared for the inevitable questions. Your social worker wants to know you are sorry about what you did, made a sincere effort to compensate for it, and are unlikely ever to repeat your mistake.

Personality Evaluation

Some states and agencies require that you complete a personality profile to establish your stability. These are not pass-or-fail tests; they are merely indicators. If you do take one, you'll probably find that it is fun and educational.

Often, in lieu of testing, you will be asked to describe yourself, what matters to you, what doesn't, what your strengths and weaknesses are. If you are infertile, have you resolved your feelings of anger and resentment?

Remember that personality is a critical factor in a home study. Your caseworker wants to gain insight into who you are and how you think.

SUMMARY

In this section your caseworker summarizes impressions and findings and recommends whether you should be given a written recommendation to adopt. Usually the report is broken down into categories much like those outlined in this chapter.

Some states require that you be given a copy of the home study. In others, although not required to do so by law, your social worker will share the findings with you as a matter of course. You may or may not know what your references have said about you. If you do not receive a copy of the results, feel free to ask for them.

Almost always, these home studies are positive. Look at the sample at the back of this book, and you will realize that, despite the probing, the final report tends to be mild, factual and complimentary.

If you are turned down, there is nothing to prevent

you from trying again. If it is not for extreme cause, such as a criminal conviction, it is entirely likely a different social worker will have a different perspective.

All states have rules regarding a new home study after a negative report. In some states, an adoptive parent may be able to get a home study through another agency right away. Other states may require a waiting period before reapplication.

Special Issues for Nontypical Adoptive Parents

In addition to the considerations raised previously in this chapter for all potential adopters, certain categories of adopters face other questions and challenges as discussed below.

Single Adopters

Like others who don't fit the ideal parent profile, you will need to be more flexible than the twenty-five-year-old couple. More and more birth mothers are involved in choosing the adoptive family. Because she wants her baby to have a better life than she could provide, she is unlikely to opt for a single parent, and there are many couples who want babies.

However, if you are willing to be more compromising on the type of child you will accept, and if you are willing to wait a bit longer, there is no reason you can't adopt. The trend is toward more non-traditional adoptions, including ones by single parents.

You might explore independent adoptions, or adoptions of an older, minority, or handicapped child, as well as foreign sources.

In addition to the questions listed earlier in this chapter, you probably will be asked some along these lines:

- What are your thoughts about single parenting?
- What experiences, if any, have you had in trying to have a child naturally or by adoption?
- What resources have you used to prepare to become a single parent?
- What are your reactions to the adoption plans of others?
- How do you handle other people's reactions to single adopters?
- What resources and support systems would you use after placement of your baby?
- Are you a homosexual? If so, describe your lifestyle.
- What are your feelings about the opposite sex?
- What are your past and present dating and relationship experiences?
- Are you currently involved in one relationship? Will that person have a substantial relationship with the child? Would you consider living with someone without being married?
- What are your feelings about marriage?
- What role models of the opposite sex will you provide for your child?
- Can you describe your parenting skills and the areas you wish to improve upon as a single parent?

You will want to demonstrate that you have a balance of interests, so you won't become obsessive about your child or, the other extreme, neglectful. Show that you have a good child-care plan, that you have friends of the opposite sex who will take an active interest in your child, and that you have married friends with whose children your child can play.

Be careful about endorsing non-traditional lifestyles to your caseworker. Although many couples live together without being married, most caseworkers would not find this arrangement acceptable.

Non-white Adopters

The majority of would-be adopters are Caucasian. But there are many infants available to black, Asian, Indian or other adopters, and more minority adopters are needed. (See the Information Guide at the back of this book to identify some sources.)

Over-Forty Adopters

Some agencies won't accept applicants over age forty. Many agencies will only place a special-needs child with you, although there are important exceptions. Some foreign sources, for example, prefer parents over forty. You can also try independent adoptions.

RECOMMENDATION TO ADOPT/POSITIVE HOME STUDY

Depending on the jurisdiction in which you will adopt, you may need a court's, an adoption agency's, or a licensed social worker's approval that you are acceptable to adopt. Typically this includes a home study. In most cases, you must be approved *before* you can be placed with a child. If you are working with an agency, this will be coordinated for you. If you are adopting through a private source or an attorney, ask him or her. Or call the state official in charge of adoptions and ask what your state requires.

Quite possibly, you are stunned by the volume of work involved in adopting. However, if you approach it systematically, progressively and logically, you will master it—just as hundreds of thousands of others have.

One of the reasons for the enormously high success rate of U.S. adoptions is the very preparation that is overwhelming you now. You are thinking through things that all parents should consider. If you are a couple, you probably are strengthening your relationship and your understanding of one another, too.

So bear up. Keep this book by your side. Read others (see the Information Guide at the back of this book for recommended titles). Keep talking to your contacts. And persevere. When you have adopted, this stage will blend into one happy blur.

CHAPTER FIVE

What Else Should You Do Before Adopting?

You have no way of knowing when your child will arrive. You may have a week's notice. You may have an hour. Prepare for that child now, while there is time. Know it is normal to be upset and anxious at times.

You have learned how to adopt. But how much do you understand about "family" itself—about children? There are many things to know and many ways to learn more about children, adoption, and parenting while you wait.

Think about the ways you can prepare yourself for the adoption in your personal life. If you have unfinished business that you have not made time to complete, then make time before your child arrives. Finish planting your garden. Make an appointment with your dentist to fill your cavities. Paint your house, and get your car tuned. These are chores that must be completed before or after the child arrives. You will be more relaxed and certainly happier if your personal life is in order. Many couples take one last vacation alone together because they know there will be a new time-consuming member of their family.

GENERAL PREPARATION

- If you haven't been around children or babies much, get acquainted with as many as you can. Offer to baby-sit. In other words, practice. When it comes time to change, feed, or bathe your own baby, you'll be more relaxed.
- Come to terms with your infertility anguish, if that's a reason for adopting. Support groups can help. Resolve, for example, has chapters nationwide.
- Obtain general counseling for adoptive parents. Many agencies mandate such counseling and offer it in-house. Usually, the counseling is offered in a group format, and considerable time is devoted to answering your questions. If, after completing the group sessions, you have any lingering questions, arrange for more counseling.

If you are not comfortable with the key issues discussed in this book, then you don't have sufficient education in the subject of adoptive parenting. No excuses. It's your responsibility to seek out more information at this stage.

If you are adopting privately, pursue your own counseling. Begin with your adoption facilitator and then branch out until you have located a reputable counselor. Even though you are not adopting through them, the top local agencies in your state are an excellent resource.

If you are in a remote area, supplement an occasional counseling session with reading. Numerous books and articles have been written in recent years (see the Information Guide at the back of this book). Set aside specific reading times.

These resources are available, and appropriate, to you. Don't skimp. Counseling will ground you throughout your parental roller coaster. You will understand what issues will arise and have a sense of how to deal with them.

• Talk to other adoptive parents. Once the word about your adopting is out, you will find that a lot of other people you know have adopted. Talk to them. Most adoptive parents enjoy helping others work through the process.

• If you are planning to adopt a foreign child, an older child, a child of another race, or a special-needs child, talk to people who have done so (see the sections on foreign or special-needs adoptions in Chapter Two).

• Consider the type of contact you will have with the birth parents of your child (see Chapter Seven). You may be able to participate in a totally closed adoption, if that's what you want. More likely, you will commit to at least some type of communication with the birth mother, even if your privacy is protected by your agency or your attorney acting as intermediary.

• Seek help if you believe there may be a problem during a future home study. If you have a history of drug abuse, see a psychiatrist. If you were arrested for drunken driving three years ago, deal with it now.

• Locate a pediatrician to care for your child. You can ask friends for recommendations, but don't stop there. Interview several. Find out the attitude of each physician about adopting. How accessible is he? What if you have a midnight emergency? Will he be available on short notice, if you need to talk or meet with him before taking your child home? (If your adoptive child is a baby, would he be willing to talk with the birth mother's pediatrician to work through any problems in the hospital?) Do you like him? Remember, you will be dealing with your pediatrician throughout the years your child is growing up.

• Look around your home. Be sure you are physically prepared for a child.

• Buy some basics, including clothes, furnishings, and food. If you are adopting a baby, the hospital will provide you with a bundle of baby things and a schedule of your baby's eating and sleeping habits for the first days at home, plus some information on general care. If adopting an older child, make sure you get the same kind of information from his caretaker (see the section on special-needs adoptions in Chapter Two). Get every detail you can, including favorite toys.

• Identify ongoing support groups you can tap into after your child arrives.

• As you educate yourself, educate those around you, especially your family. If you already have a child, explain the adoption as clearly as you can. Understand that your child probably will be ambivalent. Remember that children under age five have a foreshortened sense of time, so don't tell them too far ahead.

• Check with your insurance company to make sure all is in order, unless you've already had to do this for the agency or home study.

• Check your employer's benefits policy to find out whether adopting parents are afforded the same leave as birth parents.

• Start thinking about baby-sitters. As you will find, they are scarce commodities.

• Decide now how you will handle the first days with your child. (If you're adopting a baby, will you be going to the hospital to pick the infant up?) Who will be with you when you first see your child? Most opt for the immediate family, including children. The more you include your birth child in the adoption, the easier the transition, even if that means taking a small child with you to another state to pick up the new family member.

• Decide what you want to take with you when you pick up the child. Remember a camera and decide who will take the pictures.

• Begin a journal (or baby book, if your child is a

newborn or infant), so your child will have mementos of his or her life with you. You may want to include pictures of the agency, your home-study report if you have it, other special events that led to the adoption.

PREPARATION FOR A NEWBORN OR INFANT

• Buy the following:

1. A car seat. It is required by law in many states.
2. A crib (and a bassinet, if the baby is a newborn).
3. Baby formula. You don't need much. Some will be provided by the hospital, and your baby may have specific dietary requirements.
4. One or two outfits for the baby. Remember, you probably will not know the sex or exact age ahead of time.
5. Diapers.

• Know where your baby will sleep. Some superstitious couples believe it's bad luck to decorate a baby's room ahead of time. At the least, make some choices and gather information on some basic furnishings.

• Attend infant-care classes. There are probably some in your area geared to adopting parents. Check with your agency, or with other agencies. Most hospitals offer some type of newborn-care program. Or call your local information-referral service.

• You may want to consider breast-feeding. Yes, adoptive mothers can breast-feed, and many think it enhances bonding. La Leche League is a good source here, because of their belief in the benefits of breast-feeding. If you do want to breast-feed, be in touch early, because it requires a good deal of work and planning.

• Be prepared to react to a complicating factor after the birth of your baby. Maybe your baby turns out to be twins. Perhaps he or she has a cleft palate. There could be a variety of unanticipated problems.

• Finally, decide on a name.

Be sure to know your agency's policy about the signing of consent forms and the placement of a baby with you. Usually, you will have at least two or three days' notice before the birth mother signs initial consent forms releasing the baby to your care. Sometimes, placement is postponed for up to six months before the consents and other legal matters—such as the birth father's rights—are finalized. In fact, many agencies send newborns to foster-care homes while the birth father's rights are being terminated.

If you have any input into the process, opt to have your baby sooner than later. The odds of a disruption are minuscule once the consent forms are signed. However, if the father's rights are being disputed in court by a contesting birth father, then you may not want the child until you know for certain that he is yours.

• Don't forget that, by most estimates, over half of

all birth mothers change their minds, keep their babies and never sign a consent for adoption placement. This is particularly devastating when you are adopting privately or openly and have begun to identify with a birth mother. She has chosen you. And you have come to view her as your child's personal caretaker before the adoption.

Know the odds and try to prepare yourself for this possibility.

ONGOING CONTACT WITH AN AGENCY

• Participate in programs required or suggested by your agency. In addition to general counseling, some agencies require people on their lists to house a birth mother (not of the specific child they are adopting). Others enlist prospective parents in fund-raising.

• Try to develop a relationship with key agency staff. Even if volunteering isn't required, it is a good idea to offer your time at the agency so you have the opportunity to get to know staff members and watch how they work.

• Look realistically for signs of a no-win situation. What if an agency can't produce? Be smart enough to investigate and, if necessary, to cut your losses before sacrificing more time, energy, money, and hope.

Go back to your agency representative and ask the following questions:

1. How long are we going to wait?
2. Will we get the type of child we want?
3. How many people are ahead of us?
4. Are you placing as many children as when we joined your program?
5. Are there significant changes in your agency's philosophy?
6. Are we scheduled for a home study?

If you receive vague answers to these critical questions, beware. On the other hand, don't harass your agency unless you have solid reason to believe you're being put off.

Your agency may be so busy placing children that it simply doesn't have the staff to answer the questions of all its waiting couples and tend to the business of adoption at the same time. It is appropriate to contact your state's adoption-licensing agency for any information it may have. If you feel there will be no placement within a reasonable time, look elsewhere.

CHAPTER SIX

Knowing the Law: Protect Your Adoption

You are expected to know the law. Period. Ignorance will not excuse or protect you. Not only do state laws differ, but so do the facts of each adoption. You should know enough about the law to be able to speak intelligently with your attorney or agency about the legal risks that you face.

Although not all states require you to have a lawyer, you're better off with one to help you wend your way through the legal maze. There is no such thing as an adoption without legal procedures. And you do not want to lose the baby later because of a legal technicality.

These are the legal steps involved in an adoption, listed in the order in which they usually happen:

CONTRACTUAL ARRANGEMENTS

Agencies and lawyers may ask you to sign a contract describing how you will work together and what the fees will be.

Lawyers, particularly, often require up-front retainers that are not tied to the actual adoption. If the birth parents back out, you may be liable for all legal fees incurred. Be aware of any clauses that require you to assume costs of medical and legal bills. Even though the birth parents may say that they are committed to the adoption when they sign a guarantee of payment for hospital bills, delivery charges, and legal fees, you'll experience a financial—as well as emotional—shock if the birth parents decide to keep the child and are unable to reimburse you for their medical expenses.

Your lawyer might tell you that you have nothing to worry about; the birth mother has made up her mind. Wrong. You *always* have something to worry about. In an independent adoption, understand that you may be asked to risk thousands of dollars with no guarantee of adoption.

If a lawyer charges a fee of, say, $100 to $200 an hour, find out what the minimum and maximum charges are. It is easy to pile up a bill of $2,000 to $10,000 and still not have a baby—or any prospects.

Determine what is included in the fees and what you will be expected to pay for over and above that. Most adoption lawyers will quote a maximum *fee* for the adoption. Later, you might find that the fee does not include the separate hearings for the termination of the biological father's legal rights or the pre-adoption guardianship hearing. If these hearings are contested, your legal fees can be double or triple the original quote.

What kinds of expenses, if any, must you assume for the birth mother? Will you be paying for living expenses and missed work? Birth-mother support can easily add up to several thousand dollars a month during the pregnancy. Remember, some states prohibit any payments to the birth mother for living expenses, missed work, and even medical expenses. Make sure you know the law. If you break it, your adoption is at risk.

CONFLICT OF INTEREST

Be certain everyone's legal rights are protected. Say, for example, your lawyer is also representing the birth mother. After she has placed the baby with you, she comes back to him and says, "You're my lawyer. I want my baby back." If the lawyer says it's too late, he may be suspected of having a conflict of interest.

Because adoptions are not usually adversarial proceedings, there is rarely a conflict. But when you see a lawyer, ask him whom he represents and what his relationship is, if any, to the birth parents. There must be a full and frank disclosure to you and the birth parents when you share a lawyer. Find out whether the birth parents were offered their own independent legal counsel. If you have any reason to suspect that the birth parents are receiving undue pressure to place the child for adoption, then logic demands that they be provided with their own lawyer.

ACCEPTABILITY TO ADOPT

Depending on your state, when the court, licensed agency or licensed social worker has approved you as qualified, potential parents who have met the set conditions to that date, you are acceptable to adopt. Acceptability to adopt usually follows, or is included within, a written home study. In most states, before being considered for placement and before any legal action can be taken, you must be legally approved as acceptable to adopt.

There are significant exceptions. In the state of New York, for example, both the home study and the supervisory study are completed, and thus the acceptability to adopt is issued, *after* placement of your child with you.

Typically, the following are needed when you apply for approval to adopt.

- Completed agency application with pictures.
- Fingerprints.

- Physician statements.
- Autobiography.
- Resumé.
- Financial statements.
- Legal arrangements.
- Fees.
- Favorable home study.

LEGAL CONSENT

Consents to Adopt (also known as surrenders) are the papers that must be signed by the birth parents (or just the birth mother, if the father is unknown) before your baby may be placed in your home. Generally, the Consent-to-Adopt papers will include:

- The name of the birth mother and the birth father. In many states, the courts will have a method of protecting confidentiality so that the adoptive parents cannot find out the names or addresses of the birth parents.
- The date and place of birth.
- The names of the adoptive parents (fictitious if this is a closed adoption).
- In some states, a legal name for the baby. Usually, the papers will say something like, "Baby Girl Sunshine is being adopted by Jane and John Doe."
- An affidavit that says the adoption is not by individuals who are relatives by blood or marriage (for whom there are different rules).

• A statement that the adoption is irrevocable, unless the state where you adopt allows rescission within a specified period.

• An itemized listing of everything paid for in connection with the adoption and any payments promised in the future.

• If applicable in your state, a statement that the birth mother has received counseling and/or legal counsel.

• If necessary, an affidavit that says the birth mother signed the consent forms as a minor. Her parent or guardian must countersign.

• Verification that the consents were signed and dated in front of a notary public and/or a judge and/or witnesses, depending on the requirements of your state.

• A statement that the consents were signed voluntarily, without fraud, duress, or undue influence of drugs or alcohol.

• A statement that, according to one or more witnesses, the birth parents appear to be signing the consents voluntarily and without coercion or undue influence, and that they are mentally sound and able to understand the consequences of their actions.

The consents are signed as soon as state law permits, usually within three to four days after birth. As is the case with virtually every adoption procedure, state laws differ.

Valid consents mean that your baby is legally entrusted to your care, or that of a foster home, pending completion of the adoption. Some states require that a guardianship hearing be held. In most, the signing of the consents is sufficient to confer guardianship.

Formal legal work can begin only after the consents have been signed. Signing of these documents does not complete the adoption, but it is a critical step to conclusion.

Once an adoption is final, birth parents can't change their minds or amend the documents they signed. Nor can they set conditions for the adopters. In other words, the courts will not approve an adoption with strings attached. In most states it is against public policy to add conditions to an adoption. Birth parents give up all legal rights to the child when they sign the consent forms, which are court-approved. The consents are not conditional. For example, birth parents and adoptive parents may agree to exchange pictures and letters before the adoption takes place. However, should the adoptive parents change their minds after the adoption, the adoption will not be reviewed or overturned by a court.

PETITION FOR TEMPORARY CUSTODY AND GUARDIANSHIP

This allows you to have your baby with you before the adoption is completed. In some states, the agency grants this custody. Other states require a court hearing. In some states, the consents alone can confer guardianship. Follow your state's laws precisely. It can be dangerous not to do so. This petition means that you are legally responsible for your baby.

RESCISSION OF CONSENT

In many states, there is no such thing. If the consent is signed properly, then it is irrevocable. In others, birth parents have a certain time in which to change their minds after signing the consent forms.

This gives the birth mother or father an opportunity to correct what could be a lifelong mistake. The argument against this procedure is that it is pointless to have the initial consents if they can be so easily rescinded. Why put the birth parents and the adoptive couple through the decision twice? Why put the adoptive parents on hold?

TERMINATION OF PARENTAL RIGHTS

If both birth parents have not consented to the adoption and signed the consents, there will be a legal Termination of Parental Rights. This must be done before you can legally adopt. In some states, the Termination of Parental Rights is done in a court hearing. In others, it is included with the consent forms. It may be voluntary or involuntary.

In a voluntary termination hearing, the birth parents almost always appear before the court. Some states may require the mother's presence but not the father's; they may accept his signed consent or affidavit instead.

In an involuntary termination, a birth parent's rights are legally terminated, usually after a specified period, for any of a number of reasons. Most often it is the birth father who loses his rights, either because he is unknown or because he abandons his baby by not offering support of any kind during the specified time, usually within one to six months after the legal documents have been filed.

Some states include Termination of Parental Rights as part of the consent process—when birth parents go voluntarily before the court or, in rare cases, when one birth parent signs an affidavit explaining why the other birth parent has not signed a consent. This generally happens when one parent has disappeared or abandoned the child.

Usually, people think of termination as having to do solely with the birth father. But mothers' rights can be terminated on the same basis. Cases of abandonment by the mother do occur. A mother might also forfeit her rights if she has been in jail or has physically abused a child.

In the court's eyes, when you adopt and gain the rights to parent, it means someone else is giving up those rights. The court wants to weigh both sets of rights. Our system gives priority to birth parents' rights—if they want them. So termination is a critical step.

INVOLUNTARY TERMINATION OF BIRTH-FATHER RIGHTS

Until the past ten to fifteen years, most birth-fathers' rights were terminated involuntarily, without their involvement, whether they wished it or not, whether they knew about their baby or not. Even today, in some cases, only a token effort is made to locate the birth father.

Yet a new awareness of birth parents' rights is beginning to affect the rights of birth fathers. In *Stanley* v. *Illinois* (405 U.S. 645, 92 S.Ct. 1208, 31 L.Ed. 2d 551 [1972]), the U.S. Supreme Court said that the rights of birth fathers are equal to those of birth mothers. Today if there has been the slightest contact with, or hint of interest in, his baby by the birth father, the judge probably will refuse to terminate his parental rights.

Over the past ten years, the courts in most states have offered more protection to birth fathers by requiring that every legal effort be made to locate a birth father.

Most states say that the birth father forfeits his rights after a specified period, under certain conditions:

- The birth father's whereabouts is unknown.

You'll need an affidavit attesting to your efforts to locate the father. If the judge is not satisfied, he will not terminate the father's rights, and the adoption cannot take place.

The best notice is informing the birth father personally of the impending adoption. At the minimum, if a birth father's name and whereabouts are unknown, all states require that you advertise for a time in a newspaper in the area where you have good reason to believe the birth father lives or in the state and county where the baby is to be adopted. Check your state's law regarding notice by publication.

In cases where a father's identity is known but his whereabouts is not, some agencies and lawyers hire private investigators to check motor-vehicle, utility, and other records. They may begin with a last-known address or a previous employer, or by contacting friends and relatives who can direct them to the birth father.

Virtually all states are tightening their laws. In more and more cases, publication is not enough, if the father can be personally served with papers notifying him of the pending adoption. He may legitimately ask the court to reopen the case or deny the adoption altogether if he can prove he was not given proper notice.

If the birth mother is married at the conception or delivery of the baby, in most states there is a strong legal presumption that the husband is the father.

In such a case, the husband must be given some type of notice that the baby is being considered for adoption. Unless he signs the consents or an affidavit of denial of paternity, he will be presumed to have legal rights to his baby.

- The father is known but there are extenuating circumstances. Perhaps he is in jail or has physically abused the baby. In cases like these, the baby probably will be adopted, depending on the type of crime committed, the length of prison sentence, or the extent of abuse.

• The father cannot be identified. This means the name and address of the father are unknown to the mother; he cannot receive personal notice of the adoption.

Reasons include:

1. The birth mother was raped by a stranger.

2. The birth mother may have met the birth father only once; she may not know his name or how to find him.

3. The birth mother was under the influence of alcohol or drugs at the time of conception, so she may not remember who the father is.

4. The mother has had more than one sexual partner.

It is not enough for the birth mother to say, "I have slept with three men, and I don't know who made me pregnant." Each of the three men must be notified of his possible fatherhood and the impending adoption.

5. The birth mother knows who the father is but refuses to identify him. Many state courts will not accept a "refusal to identify." Some do, but usually the birth mother must sign an affidavit or go under oath in court and say that the father is aware of the pregnancy and has taken some action proving he wants nothing to do with the baby. This often means a threat of violence.

He may warn, "You involve me, and you'll be sorry for it."

Or perhaps the birth father is married to someone else. He says, "I don't want anyone to know about this. If you tell, you will be in serious trouble."

Or he gets scared and defensive. "How are you going to prove I'm the father? I'm going to deny it."

In some cases, the court will say that the birth mother's reason for refusing to identify the birth father isn't good enough. These birth mothers must explain their situations before the courts.

Several states, such as New York, Oregon, and Utah, are establishing birth-father registries in which a father can sign up to establish a legal claim to his baby. In effect, the registry requires him to take affirmative action if he wants to keep his child. It eliminates the need for the court to seek out the birth father actively or to reopen a case if he comes forward after an adoption is completed.

Technically, the registry concept solves the problem of notice—but only if a birth father knows about his baby and the registry.

Although statistics are incomplete, up to 40 percent of birth fathers are unknown today, generally for the reasons described above. Those who are known usually cooperate in the adoption because they fear being exposed, because they want nothing more to do with the birth mother or the baby, or because they are too young or too poor to take on the responsibility of parenthood.

In most cases, if a father knows about the pregnancy and wants to parent his child, he will become involved before the baby's birth. For older children, the court can readily determine whether the father is actively participating in the child's life.

PETITION TO ADOPT

This is your legal request to the court asking that your adoption be completed. Filing this petition means that you have finished all of the steps legally required of you at this point in the proceedings.

At this stage, you usually have custody of the baby, although formal guardianship (required in some states) and/or termination of guardianship (required in some states) and/or termination of parental rights may or may not have been completed.

The Petition to Adopt usually includes the following kinds of information:

- Sex of baby.
- Time, date, and place of birth.
- Your names, address, and ages.
- Type of adoption. The court wants to know whether the birth parents are related by blood or marriage to the adopting parents or if it is a step-parent adoption.
- A statement that you have conformed with the ap-

propriate state laws and requirements for placement of the baby.

Recently, the mother of a birth mother came in to our agency and told us that a friend wanted to adopt her daughter's baby. The plan her daughter and her daughter's friend worked out didn't sound right to her. The birth mother was to check into the hospital under the name of the adoptive mother. That way, the baby would have the adopter's name right away, plus be insured under the adopting mother's policy, so the hospital bills would be paid. No one in the hospital would know the difference.

The mother of the pregnant woman was right. It is a crime to adopt under fraudulent circumstances. And there would be a second felony in this case, the fraud against the insurance company.

• A list of all expenses incurred. In most states, your expenses are scrutinized if you are not adopting through a licensed adoption agency. Allowable expenses fluctuate dramatically among states. Some states will not complete your adoption until every bill has been paid and reported.

• A statement that you feel you are fit and proper people to adopt. This usually includes some information about your marriage and your lifestyle.

• A request to change the baby's name to the new legal name you have chosen.

• A statement about the home study. In some states, you will have been approved previously by the court or your agency as acceptable to adopt and will have undergone a home study before the placement of your baby with you. In other states, the home study is combined with the supervisory study and completed after placement.

- A list of any unusual medical problems.
- Termination information, if applicable.
- A statement about the status of the birth father.

The Petition to Adopt is filed before the actual hearing at which your adoption is completed. The time between filing the Petition and the hearing date is subject to differing state rules.

POST-PLACEMENT SUPERVISORY STUDY

All courts require some sort of follow-up study after your child is placed with you but before the adoption is completed. In most states, you already will have received a favorable home study report. In some states, there will be a combination home study and post-placement report. The purpose of the supervisory study is to validate your adoption to the courts—not, as so many fear, to find an excuse to take your baby away. This can be a time to gain support, ask questions, gather additional information, and brainstorm with someone qualified and experienced in adoption. Remember, your social worker wants to do everything possible to make your adoption work.

A supervisory study is conducted anytime within one year after placement. It consists of up to five visits to your home, each lasting anywhere from a half hour to several hours.

There usually is more than one visit; your social worker wants to see you at different times as your family evolves. Often, the same social worker who conducted your home study also will be responsible for your supervisory study. When an older child is involved, there will generally be several visits between the child and the adoptive parents so that a proper transition can be made between homes before the child makes a permanent move.

Whether or not you have discussed it before, your social worker probably will bring up the question of punishment. If you say, "I don't see anything wrong with spanking a child," you are going to elicit a raised eyebrow. Your social worker may ask you to participate in further counseling.

He or she will want to determine whether any problems have developed—if, for example, bonding is not occurring smoothly, or your baby has any physical problems. Are your house and neighborhood safe? Are you doing well? Are you fulfilling your obligation to provide a good home, medical assistance, food, shelter, clothing, love, and support? Are you happy? In short, your social worker wants a picture of your new family.

Typically your social worker will want to know some of the following:

- How you and your spouse are dealing with one another. Do you spend less time with each other than before your baby came? Do you make time for just the two of you? Is your relationship strained? Is there any competition in caring for the baby?

- How you feel about your child. Perhaps you adopted a ten-year-old boy who is mentally disabled. Is the reality what you expected? Are there any surprises or second thoughts?
- Who the primary caretaker is. What is your division of care?
- Whether you have taken your child to the doctor. What were the results?
- What changes you have experienced with your other children. How have you handled those changes?
- How the other siblings have reacted and whether your child has been accepted by the rest of your family.
- What your day-to-day routine is.
- How you have responded to your baby's needs. And he to yours.
- How you are handling logistics such as baby-sitters. Have you been out without the baby? Any trips? Has the mother gone back to work? Are you attending church?
- Whether there are any problems or signs of trouble. One couple postponed naming their baby. In

> fact, they were having trouble bonding with him. Once they understood there was a problem, they went for counseling. It helped, and the result was a happy one.

Your social worker will want to help you work through the attitude, "I am so lucky to have this child. I have got to be a superhuman parent." Not so. In fact, you are setting yourself up for failure. When you begin to think of yourselves as normal parents, when you realize mistakes and problems are inevitable, then things will become much easier.

Most studies are quite comprehensive, building on your earlier home study. Your social worker is looking for more than verbal answers to questions asked. He or she is intent on watching how your family works.

Be aware that you are, in fact, being observed, even as the conversation progresses. If your baby needs to be changed or fed, who does it? How do the other siblings interact? Is there anything unusual in the way either one of you handles your baby? If your baby cries, is he attended to?

Does the husband spend all his time on the phone, while the wife takes care of the baby? Is it his baby, too? Or just hers? Although most unlikely, if the social worker feels the father is a mere observer, the judge could delay completing the adoption and ask for more information.

If you have questions or doubts, this is the time to resolve them. There's usually no need to be afraid to disagree with your social worker or to ask for help and suggestions. However, if you have any doubts about confiding possible problems to the social worker, then don't. But don't go without help. As you now know, there are many places to turn. Remember, most problems are solvable. And the overwhelming percentage of adoptions are huge successes.

If you have sound reason to believe you may receive a negative report, take action. Ask for a second study by a different social worker. Do not risk your future on an aberration.

In a small number of cases, usually with special-needs placements, there *are* unsolvable problems. This is the time, in a postplacement study, that any such problem should surface. You may be trapped into a situation that you cannot cope with. If so, do your best, and then move on.

You may also be in one of the rare situations in which the court recommends against adoption. To repeat: A negative supervisory report is most unusual, triggered only by the most severe situations—filth, malnourishment, neglect, abuse, hostility, advanced drug abuse, police reports of family fights that endanger your baby. Abuses that would prompt the court to disrupt your adoption are the same ones that would cause the court to remove a baby who was born to you. Unfit parents are measured by the same criteria, regardless of whether the baby is adopted.

The older or more disabled the child, and the less informed you are about the process, the greater the risk of a disruption.

WAITING

It can be upsetting to learn that, for whatever reason, there will be a delay. And a procedural delay—one with absolutely no bearing on the merits of your adoption—is not uncommon.

Some agencies automatically put an adoption on hold if all the paperwork is not completed. Other agencies will not allow your adoption to be completed until all bills are paid. Or the court may postpone the completion if there are any questions about excessive payments.

In some difficult cases, the adoptive parents themselves may request a postponement because they are not certain whether the adoption will work. Generally, this happens with special-needs children, where time is needed to explore the relationship. Most parents want the adoption completed the minute they meet their baby.

Be certain that if your baby comes from one state and you live in another, you have complied fully with the requirements prescribed by the Interstate Compact laws (described later in this chapter) that govern across-state-lines adoptions.

FINAL HEARING

By this time, any problems have been resolved. If anything were going to disrupt your adoption, you would know it.

The final hearing completes your adoption. All required reports have been filed, all conditions met. Any challenge to the adoption would have been made long before, usually at the time of Termination of Parental Rights.

The final hearing for the Order of Adoption is generally held within six months after your child is placed with you. It varies, however. In Maryland, for example, the wait for completion is only fifteen days.

The hearing, which is confidential and closed to the public, takes place in the judge's chambers or in a closed courtroom. It lasts anywhere from five to thirty minutes, and the judge will ask you questions along the following lines:

- Have you completed all payments and made a full accounting to the court?
- Have you finished all your paperwork?
- Why do you feel you are fit and proper people to adopt?
- Is there anything that would disqualify you from adopting?
- Is there anything else the court should know regarding this adoption?

When the judge is satisfied that all the information is complete and that your answers are satisfactory, and if the adoption is uncontested (as in almost every case), the Order for Adoption is issued.

If the birth father contests the adoption or if a significant illegality surfaces, an adoption could be contested. Almost always, this sort of challenge is dealt with well ahead of the final hearing. Frankly, it is very unlikely that a judge is going to take your baby away without extreme provocation. Should there be a contested adoption, there would be a court trial.

Understand that you will not walk out of the hearing with your Order of Adoption and the birth certificate. You will receive them in the mail in a few months. But, legally, your adoption is final. You are a family.

ADOPTION DISRUPTION

A disruption may occur before an adoption is legally completed, prior to the final adoption order.

If you have committed an illegal act in adopting, or if a birth parent presses a legitimate claim, the court can stop the adoption. Fewer than one percent of baby adoptions are disrupted, although, as has been mentioned before, the numbers increase with troubled, older or special-needs children.

If the court finds out that you paid someone off, or that the adoption occurred under an assumed name, or that there was some form of coercion, there could be a legal disruption.

If the birth father appears and says, "No one told me my child was being adopted," it's usually enough to reopen the case. In a few states, the court might decide to disrupt the adoption. Other states use the "best interest of the child" test, which usually favors the adoptive parents:

"Where were you when the birth mother was pregnant? We think it is in the best interest of the child not to disrupt this adoption."

In situations where a family has not bonded or there are severe medical and/or mental problems that the parents cannot cope with, adopting parents can withdraw the Petition to Adopt until the moment the final adoption order is drawn.

The appropriate state agency can disrupt the adoption if it finds evidence of abuse, malnutrition, or abhorrent living conditions.

According to a recent study at the University of Southern Maine, disruption causes are often complex. There may be several: a mismatch; a lack of preparation, either by the family or the agency; inadequate attachments; lack of appropriate postplacement services; lack of family resources; an overloaded or strained family system; or insurmountable obstacles, such as health or mental problems.

THE INTERSTATE COMPACT

There is no nationwide uniformity in adoption law; however, all states participate in the Interstate Compact, which regulates interstate adoptions.

Each participating state has an Interstate Compact Administrator (ICA), whose job it is to facilitate adoption placements into and out of his state. An adoption in which the adopting parents and the adoptee live in different states must be approved by the ICA in both states. The ICA reviews home studies and medical and social histories to verify that the placement is a good one and in the best interests of the baby.

You may not transport an adopted baby across state lines until you have the approval of the Interstate Compact Administrators from the sending and receiving states. Otherwise you are taking substantial risk and the adoption could be overturned at a later date.

An interstate adoption involves still more paperwork. The *ICPC 100 form*—ICPC stands for Interstate Compact on the Placement of Children—requires the following information:

- Background of the adopting couple.
- Names of the agencies or adoption supervisors in both states.
- Name, address, and complete social and medical history of the birth parents, if known.
- Projected date of birth or complete information on the child.
- Accounting of all adoption fees.
- Agency license and/or attorney license.
- A completed home study.
- Copies of the consents after they have been signed.

Generally, the receiving state is in control; it is up to the administrators from both the sending and receiving states to decide whether the child can cross state lines for the purpose of adoption. Legally, a state has thirty days in which to respond to a request to bring in an adopted child.

Often you may have to wait a week or two before the compact administrator allows you to take your child back into your home state. Many states will not even allow you to see your child prior to compact approval, to protect you against bonding with a child that is still not yours.

A word of warning if you are adopting across state lines through an attorney or nonaligned facilitator: Be prepared to add several thousand dollars to the cost of your adoption. If your compact administrator will not allow you to see the child before approval, then the child will have to remain in the hospital, at an average cost of approximately $250 per day, or the child will be placed in foster care with a licensed agency that will probably charge you extra as well. Virtually every licensed adoption agency in the country doing interstate placements has a license for foster care. These agencies will provide proper care during the waiting period, but remember, your child may be two weeks old before you first see him, depending on your state's policy.

If you are adopting privately, be aware that many licensed agencies refuse to work with attorneys or nonlicensed facilitators. Those agencies that do are often understaffed, and they may not have homes available when needed. Furthermore, an inexperienced attorney who has had few if any dealings with interstate placements may make paperwork errors that lengthen the waiting period and increase the costs for interstate approval.

It is critical that children crossing state lines for adoption be properly approved through the interstate compact. Noncompliance can void an otherwise legal adoption. Extreme caution is required.

The wait can be infuriating. You may be frantic to get back to work; your family may be anxious. If you have custody of the child, it's tough frittering away your first days with your baby in a hotel or at a friend's home. Prepare yourself for a wait and budget for the additional costs.*

There is some question about the authority of the Interstate Compact vs. that of the state courts. If the Interstate Compact Administrator approves the adoption, he essentially is inviting you to cross state lines and enter his state. So, although the courts technically are the final adjudicators, it may be a moot point. A judge is unlikely to spoil an adoption when you and your baby are already settled in his state and the baby has been allowed in at the direction and approval of another state authority.

Do not fail in any way to comply with your state law or the Interstate Compact requirements. Your adoption can be invalidated by either entity. If you are involved with an agency or lawyer who says you don't have to comply with both, beware. You are responsible for the legality of your adoption. Don't take any chances.

*For further information on adopting across state lines, see page 243.

CHAPTER SEVEN

Learning about Birth Parents

It's only in the past few years that birth parents have become real players in the adoption game. Previously, no one paid much attention to them. A birth mother often had her baby in an unwed mothers' home while her family told everyone she was visiting relatives; birth fathers were usually completely ignored, even by the most progressive professionals.

No more. Birth parents' rights are being prioritized. As a result, the entire field of adoption is changing.

This chapter is merely an introduction into educating yourselves about birth parents. Many books have been written that explain in detail the physical and emotional changes birth parents experience during pregnancy and adoption (see reading list at the back of the book).

You are encouraged to continue your education through additional reading, personal meetings with birth parents, and adoption education in your own community. The more you understand about birth parents, the less you will fear them.

WHAT DOES THE BIRTH MOTHER EXPERIENCE DURING PREGNANCY AND ADOPTION?

Because of the secrecy about adoption over the past forty years, birth mothers have been stereotyped, and misinformation and misconceptions are rampant. Contrary to myth, the birth mother is typically wise enough to make her decision rationally. She usually knows who the father is. Further, almost all birth mothers have had an opportunity to have an abortion. They give birth for a variety of reasons: opposition to abortion, guilt, religion, hopes for marriage or a strong relationship with the father, ignorance about pregnancy.

The overwhelming majority of birth mothers are motivated by what is best for their baby, a better life than they can provide. They want to give their child two loving parents, a family life, security—and the bonus of a nice home, a college education, and perhaps the opportunity to travel or pursue a particular creative interest or hobby.

Birth mothers often are under incredible pressure to keep their babies. Others may insist that it is better to have a baby and rear him marginally than place him up for adoption. Often a mother will find the decision to place her baby the most difficult one she'll ever make. For that reason, it's imperative that she receive counseling. She should know:

- Her legal rights and those of the birth father.
- The types of services available to her before and after delivery.
- What emotions she will face before and after the placement.

Most birth mothers want to place their babies as soon as possible after delivery. Hopefully, the mother will have thought about the type of family she wants for her baby and the amount of communication with the adopting parents that would be comfortable for her (see Chapter Two for information on open adoption). Usually a match is made several weeks before delivery.

The single most difficult time for a mother is immediately after delivery. That is when she must confront her decision. Until the past few years, birth mothers rarely saw their babies—ever. Now, research into grieving and loss issues comes down strongly in favor of making that baby real to the mother, of giving her a chance to say good-bye. If the mother needs to see her baby, it is important that she do so. She may need to see that the baby is healthy, that he has all of his fingers and toes. Seeing her baby often helps reaffirm her decision.

For most birth mothers, the acute grieving period lasts at least several months. Counseling at this stage can help enormously. Many mothers grieve for decades, especially if they have not received professional counseling. Almost inevitably, birth mothers and birth fathers want their children to know that they gave them up out of love and that they will always remember them.

WHY DO BIRTH PARENTS PLACE THEIR BABIES FOR ADOPTION?

Lack of money is seldom the sole reason for placing a child for adoption. The birth parent usually can figure out a way to get the financial support he or she needs. Generally, there are other reasons as well. Here are some of the most common:

• Many realize that wanting a child and rearing a child are two different things. Many are too young and simply lack the necessary resources.

• Often, birth parents already have other children. They understand parenting and know they cannot manage another child.

"I have a three-year-old, and he's doing OK. But we are barely getting by. How am I going to split it one more way?" a relinquishing mother asks.

Almost all birth parents who have other children speak of their desire to give their child a better life and make a gift to an adoptive couple.

• Some birth parents have had a previous positive adoption experience. Some place for a second and third time.

• Some birth parents are forced to give up their babies by the state. This could be because of any number of things, including child abuse and incarceration.

HOW MUCH WILL YOU KNOW ABOUT THE BIRTH PARENTS OF YOUR BABY?

It used to be thought that the less you knew the better. That way, when your child asked you about his or her birth parents, you could honestly say, "I don't know." The less you knew, it was believed, the less it would interfere with your bonding. The more unreal the birth parents were, the more real you would become.

Some adoptive parents believe they are protecting their adopted child if they hide the fact that his or her birth parents have less-than-savory pasts. But if you leave the slate blank, your child may tend to fill it in with something worse than the truth. Studies repeatedly show that ignorance breeds more insecurity than does knowledge. And in some situations—medical emergencies, for instance, where information about a birth parent's health and illness history is vital—ignorance can be dangerous.

WHAT SHOULD YOU KNOW ABOUT THE BIRTH PARENTS?

Today, we gather more information about birth parents than ever before. And the trend to openness means that adoptive and birth parents sometimes meet. Generally, however, confidentiality is still carefully guarded. Unless you are participating in a cooperative open adoption, all the information you receive about the birth parents will be non-identifying, meaning that the birth parents and the adoptive parents cannot be readily identified or located from the information provided. Some of the information may be missing, misleading, or distorted if a birth parent chooses not to share it or if the birth father does not participate. Whether you want it now or not, gather as much information as you can. Every state requires that a minimum amount of information about health and social history be supplied, if available.

Often, because of the real possibility that a birth mother will change her mind about adoption at the last moment, you may not receive all information until the actual placement. If you are adopting a newborn and are told there is no information, ask why. Follow up. This is critical. The agency should be in touch with the birth mother and provide a substantial amount of information to you. Your baby's future, and certainly your child's peace of mind, may hinge on information about his birth parents. Many adoptive parents assume that their birth parents will be young, uneducated, destitute, and in poor health. Not so. Typically, a birth mother who places her child will be in her early twenties. She is likely to be single and working, and will have at least a high school degree.

Adoption is a responsible decision, and contrary to myth, the birth mother will very likely be a responsible and mature woman. Normally she will be cooperative in giving you as much information as possible. Likewise, out of concern for the health of their children, most birth mothers get proper prenatal care and good medical attention.

Your immediate concern will be your baby's health. Once you pass that hurdle, though, you should be concerned with long-term issues. If you can, find out the following about the birth parents:

• *Reason the child is being placed for adoption.* This is critical. If the answer is not given, try to find out why. Your child will need to understand why his birth parents decided not to parent: "Why was I different? What was it about me that made them give me up?"

The more you know, the easier it will be to explain as your child gets older and becomes inquisitive.

• *Physical description.* Try to find out the birth parents' heights, weights, color of eyes and hair, body builds, complexions, baldness, breast size, coordination, athletic ability. These are the kinds of things children want to know as they are growing up.

• *Health history.* A complete health history is critical. Are there any medical problems that could be hereditary? Any mental illness or learning disabilities? Does either birth parent drink, smoke, or use drugs?

Think about your own family. List illnesses, allergies, mental problems, alcoholism. You will quickly realize that there is no such thing as an ideal family. So make allowances, just as you would if you were giving birth.

Don't demand a perfect birth mother. Some might not have had an ideal diet. Some will have smoked during the pregnancy; approximately the same percentage of birth mothers smoke as people in the general community, and most of their babies are healthy. Maybe those babies could be bigger—smoking does affect birth weight—but the fact is that they are healthy.

Moderate alcohol intake or drug use can be considered in the same light as smoking. If the birth mother drinks or uses drugs, it does not mean the baby will automatically have medical problems, but you should be alert and have the baby checked. You should find out how much alcohol or what drugs were used and for how long. Serious drug abuse can cause problems, and, in that case, the baby should be monitored closely. In severe cases, consult with your pediatrician about drug addiction or fetal alcohol syndrome.

Because the birth mother will be concerned for her baby, you will almost always know if you have reason to worry.

• *Social history.* Type of family upbringing, neighborhood, surroundings.

• *Education/Intellect/Employment.* This can be deceptive. Don't disqualify a birth parent because he or she didn't complete high school. Many birth parents have children at a young age and drop out of school to rear them. Or perhaps they married young and needed to work. A birth mother with a college degree might not be as smart as one without a college education who survived on her wits. So look to other measures of intellect. If one of the birth parents is indeed slow, you need to know that. But don't make that judgment based solely on education levels. And, if a birth parent is not currently employed, don't automatically assume laziness is a reason.

• *Ethnic background.* Interesting to know, but not necessarily critical. A lot of people don't know their ethnic background. In the United States we have such a blending of nationalities that many people don't consider it important.

• *Other family history.* Information on any siblings and the birth parents' parents. Still living? What other family is there?

• *Religion.* This may extend to preference for the way the baby will be raised.

• *Labor and delivery.* Emotional and physical state of the birth mother during labor and delivery. Did she see and hold her baby?

• *Future contact.* This increasingly complex issue addresses the amount of future contact, if any, that the birth parents would like to have with you and/or their biological child.

WHAT WON'T YOU KNOW ABOUT THE BIRTH PARENTS OF YOUR BABY?

Usually you will know much more about the birth mother than the birth father because she generally is the one providing the information (although that is changing). Even if you don't know anything about the father, you can make some pretty reliable judgments based on what you know about the mother. Typically, they have similar backgrounds. If the mother is a college student, chances are good the father will be, as well.

Often, information about birth parents has gone through many filters. It may be wrong. Find out, if you can, the source of the information. Is everything you are told hearsay? Usually, information comes directly from the birth mother to the agency or lawyer. If the birth father does not cooperate, his background may be a guess or a patchwork of truths and untruths. In some cases, the birth mother may not be sure who the father is, so no real information is recorded.

Adoptive parents often have unrealistic expectations in terms of the specificity of the information. You have to realize that you won't know everything. There will always be additional information you will wish you had. Remember, you will know only as much as the birth parents want you to know, and that may well include some of their fantasies, good and bad.

If you are adopting through a state agency, you are

probably adopting an older child who has been in foster care. Unless the parents have disappeared, you probably will have reams of information about this kind of child—medical history, psychiatric reports, personal habits, likes and dislikes.

If you find that an agency has seriously misrepresented critical facts about your child, you have some recourse. There is liability on the part of the agency, a new trend in adoption practice. Agencies no longer can ignore critical health information or refuse to pass along medical histories.

Although you have a legal right to honesty, you cannot expect an agency to assume the role of private investigator. An agency cannot be held responsible for information that was not available. Otherwise, adoptions would be litigated out of existence.

CHAPTER EIGHT

Welcoming a New Member to Your Family

This is it. It is real. You finally will meet your baby. No one could be better prepared. Your library overflows with books on babies and adoption. You've studied and attended classes and participated in group meetings.

Depending on the laws in your state and whether you are adopting privately or through an agency, you could pick your baby up at the hospital, at your agency, or at your lawyer's office.

There can be some awkwardness when first caring for your baby. Bonding is not instantaneous. In your drive for perfection, you may overreact to any imagined symptom or abnormality. In your eagerness to feed and coddle him, you may interrupt his sleep patterns. So he may cry more than usual. It takes time to develop a routine.

There tends to be enormous ignorance about adoptive parenting. There is an idea that it is easier; you didn't go through the delivery of your baby and so you are not tired. Yet if you have a cranky or a colicky baby, you could be caught up in twenty-four-hour care, just like anyone else. Parenting is parenting.

Your support system should be in place. Use it. You have chosen your pediatrician. If he or she has a bias against adopted children, it may surface now. If you detect such an attitude, change doctors. As your child grows, your pediatrician may be your most critical resource.

Remember: In the United States, *the overwhelming majority of all newborns are relatively healthy and normal.* Of those newborns who are pronounced healthy in the hospital, *about 99 percent will remain healthy.* For that small percentage with abnormalities, there are dependable tests to determine the extent of any problem.

An Apgar test, done at birth and shortly after, determines color, heart rate, motor ability, reaction to stimulus, and other key measures of normalcy. Some states require additional tests to be taken at birth and then several months later.

If there is cause for concern—possible hereditary abnormalities or alcohol or drug abuse by the birth mother—genetic screening can be conducted on the baby as well.

Some neurological problems cannot be detected at birth. The older a child, the more definitive a neurological prognosis is likely to be. Unless you have solid cause for concern, however, there is no need to take your baby to a neurologist. In fact, resist the temptation to call in any medical specialists unless the hospital staff or your pediatrician specifically advises you to do so.

Because of the confidentiality that is maintained in most adoptions, the adoptive parents rarely speak directly with the hospital doctor who delivered the baby. If you have questions, ask your agency to help you talk to the proper experts. If there are medical problems or if the baby is premature, exceptions are made. In that case, the attending physician will want to talk to you about your baby's care. You may even decide to keep the same doctor if he has been closely managing your child's care all along.

In any case, it is a good idea to take your new baby to a pediatrician within the first two weeks, to confirm that your baby is OK, to ask all of the questions that have piled up, and to establish contact. In fact, most adoptive parents schedule their first appointment within a day or two of picking up the baby.

FOSTER CARE

Many adoption agencies place babies in foster care as a matter of course. In some cases, an undecided birth mother may not be ready to sign the adoption papers. At times there seems to be an over-reliance on foster care in adoptions where it is not indicated. In almost all infant adoptions, it is best for both the adoptive parents and the child to be together as soon as possible.

On the other hand, with older children (see Chapter Two), foster care can be a valuable transition tool, serving as a buffer until a child and his adoptive parents determine whether a match is realistic.

In a recent column, Erma Bombeck quoted a letter from one adoptive mother: "When we were adopting our daughter, the social worker shared a simple note with us from her 'foster mother' who took care of her during her first seven months. It said, 'She has allergies, can't stand squash and likes to be rocked to sleep.' "

In other words, foster parents can add an important dimension to a child's life.

NAMING YOUR CHILD

Naming your baby is a meaningful claiming gesture. Sometimes, a birth mother will already have named the baby and does not want you to change it. But you are the parent, and it is your right to name your baby, whether he or she has a name already or not. When the time comes, be certain the birth certificate includes your child's new name.

If your child is older, you probably will want to keep his name. It may be one of the few constants in his life.

Or he may want to change it to symbolize his belonging. If he is old enough, ask him what he would like to do.

THE FIRST DAYS FOR YOUR NEW FAMILY

Give yourself some time to get comfortable on your own. Have someone come in to help if you wish.

You might invite relatives over for dinner. If you are active in your church or synagogue, check on any special ceremonies. Decide what you will tell people about the adoption and what you want to keep private. Hopefully, you will have helped educate those around you about the adoption. But remember that, even if you have, they will not have your depth of understanding.

BONDING

Bonding usually occurs quickly, especially with newborns. As soon as you see your baby, you may know it was meant to be. If you do not experience the rush of love you expected, not to worry. There are as many variables as there are parents. In some cases, parents don't truly bond with their child for many days after he arrives.

One couple was devastated when their baby turned out to be undeniably ugly. It bothered the new parents so much the first day that they seriously considered having the adoption disrupted. Counseling helped them realize that their feelings were not abnormal. Within a few days, as they came to know their baby, their love took hold.

There is no single appropriate response the first time you see your baby. Some people go wild. Others take their time. Some are shy. Frequently, the adoptive parents will not know what to say or do at the first meeting, especially if they are not alone with their child. Be assured that there is no one correct behavior. There are many.

If bonding does not occur within the first few weeks, it may mean there are unresolved issues regarding adoption itself. Or it could mean the baby does not meet your expectations. If you feel you are not bonding as you should, get counseling immediately. If counseling, and time, do not make you feel comfortable, remember: No one will make you take this baby if you don't want to. There can be other choices.

If you are adopting an older child, bonding can take longer. In a recent case, a toddler did not want to be held or touched, cried constantly, and rarely laughed. She was simply not adapting. The adoptive parents brought her into the agency and explained the behavior problems to the social worker. The agency contacted the birth mother with specific questions about the child's actions. The birth mother admitted that the child had been repeatedly uprooted from home to home; the child was afraid of bonding and was protecting herself from hurt. Once the couple understood, they took a different approach with her and are now ecstatic about their little girl. The older the child, the more care you must take to introduce him gently into your life. Perhaps you should arrange several preliminary meetings for longer and longer periods until he is comfortable with you.

CHAPTER NINE

After the Adoption: Nurturing the Child and the Family

Now you can relax. It's legal. You have signed the last papers, braved the last interview, endured the final scrutiny, survived the legal maze. You are a family.

With one exception. Although the dynamics are just like those of any other family, the beginnings differ. And those beginnings will, to some degree, affect your family's future. They will create issues only adoptive families must address.

Most important, if there are problems beyond the usual, seek help. As you know by now, there is special counseling available to adoptive parents.

One other point. If you adopted because you are infertile, you probably realize that adoption does not cure infertility. Although you are no longer childless, you are still infertile. You may wonder whether you, in fact, did the right thing in adopting. Relax. As bonding occurs, the second-guessing will subside.

ANSWERING QUESTIONS FROM OTHERS ABOUT YOUR ADOPTED CHILD

People will often ask questions in front of your child as if he or she weren't there.

"Is she yours?"

"Do you have any children of your own?"

"How did you get her?"

Don't tell everyone the whole story. Later you may wish you hadn't. One answer that works nicely is: "We think that information belongs to our child, and we would like him to know about it first."

You may be angry at what you see as an intrusion into your privacy. People don't approach someone who has just given birth and ask the same kinds of questions. For some reason, people often feel adoption is everyone's business. If you are dealing with your family and close friends, take the time to educate them, to share your reading with them. Your family and friends' attitudes will affect your child over the years.

TALKING TO YOUR ADOPTED CHILD

No matter how young your child was when you adopted him, he has suffered a loss. And he must deal with it in his own way. Some say this loss is so sharp and indelible that it colors his life absolutely and irrevocably. Others argue that the adjustment is, in most cases, minor.

A child's reaction to his beginnings and what he will, at some point, interpret as a rejection, varies according to his other experiences. Inevitably, however, the questions will surface, at least in his own mind: Who am I? Who were my birth parents? Why did they decide not to keep me? What did I do wrong?

Love is not the issue. A child may fear that he will somehow be abandoned or UNadopted. A good adoption takes a childhood. You need to keep adopting your child for twenty years, reinforcing your love and your bond.

It used to be that adoptive parents brought home a baby and played out the fantasy that they were his biological parents. As long as adoption was closed, the secret could be guarded.

That option simply doesn't exist anymore. It is virtually impossible for parents to adopt in a vacuum of secrecy. If they tried, the deception would be quickly exposed, either intentionally or inadvertently. Regardless, adoption experts now come down strongly on the side of full and early sharing of adoption information with your child.

Ideally, your child should be able to say, "I cannot remember not knowing that I was adopted."

By introducing the subject early and calmly, you avoid the confrontational situations of past adoptions. Your child may not understand what adoption is when you first tell him. But as time passes, you can share more and more information until you have filled in the empty spaces.

As he grows, your child's questions will guide you. And he will interpret your answers in a new way. His reality at three is a long way from the reality of a thirteen-year-old. He may hear the words but not really understand what you are saying. Or he may simply forget. It is entirely possible that those answers are much less important to your child than they are to you.

Joey, age five, loved to hear the story about how he was adopted in Phoenix, about how he was picked up at the agency and about how exciting it was, how much his parents loved him and how important it was to them. Night after night, Joey asked to hear the story of his adoption. His parents were enthralled—pleased that their telling was so successful. One night, Joey asked, "Dad, what's a Phoenix?"

As he grows up, Joey will understand that Phoenix is not a baby factory. Children only take on what they are prepared to understand. Their response helps indicate their level of interest. You may feel compelled to tell your child every detail of his adoption at the earliest opportunity. Until he can understand it, he may be relatively uninterested or overwhelmed by the information.

According to journalist Lois Melina, who writes on adoption, "Preschoolers usually cannot differentiate between being adopted and being born into a family. To children that age, anyone who lives with them is part of the family. The reason they seem so willing to accept their adoptive status is because they don't understand it."

In the past, it was thought that the child who asked no questions was well adjusted, while the inquiring child was insecure. Today we know that is not so. Silence does not mean lack of interest. Instead, it may mean a reluctance to broach the subject with his parents, or a substitution of fantasy for reality.

If you are uncomfortable talking about adoption, your child may avoid the subject. Or he may conclude there is something bad about adoption. One of your great challenges is balance, to talk about adoption enough so that your child appreciates it and knows that it is an acceptable topic for conversation, but not to dwell on it to the point where your child begins to think there is something wrong. You want to talk about adoption frankly and forthrightly, while avoiding talk of rescuing, so your child won't have to be eternally grateful.

TALKING TO YOUR ADOPTED CHILD ABOUT BIRTH PARENTS

Parents used to try to protect their children from knowledge of their birth parents. If confronted, they would often lie.

"Your birth parents died in an accident."

"Your birth parents are completely unknown. We don't have any information about them."

So not only did the adopted children feel guilty for surviving, they also carried their questions with them, unanswered, through their lives.

You should refer to birth parents with empathy, as real people. It is important that your child understands that his birth parents loved him and found it very difficult to place him for adoption, but they thought it would be best for him. Some therapists warn against relating the adoption directly to love, as in: "Your birth parents gave you up for adoption because they loved you so much." Your child may worry that you also love him enough to place him with yet another set of parents.

Reassure your child that his parents placed him for adoption because they were not able to provide for him or parent him—not because there was anything wrong with him. Because children are so self-centered, they tend to take the blame for everything that goes wrong.

Talk about the birth father as well as the birth mother. It is easy, and common, to ignore him. Your child may be confused and think that his adoptive father is really his birth father.

Children often fantasize about their biological parents:

"Maybe my real mother was a movie star who had to give me up, but soon she will come and find me."

"What if my father is a famous congressman who doesn't know about me?"

When your child reaches his teens, share whatever information you have. If it is insufficient, offer to help fill in the gaps. Be prepared to go back to the adoption agency or lawyer who helped you adopt and do whatever you can to get more information. You might leave a letter with the agency on behalf of your child for his birth parents, indicating that you are looking for more information. Most importantly, make it clear to your child that you are not standing in his way.

Usually, teens are not interested in meeting their birth parents, just in obtaining information. Maybe they are testing you, just to see what your reaction will be. Generally, it is recommended that any meeting be postponed until your child reaches adulthood. A teenager confronting identity issues has enough confusion in his life without adding more.

COPING AS YOUR ADOPTED CHILD SEEKS AN IDENTITY

If yours is not a cooperative adoption in which you are in touch with your child's birth parents, at some point your child will have to deal with the fact that being adopted means there are questions that can't be answered by you. There is a natural curiosity to know:

"Whom do I look like?"

"Do I have any brothers and sisters I don't know about?"

"What was the real reason I was given up for adoption?"

The fact that children think these thoughts does not mean they are unhappy. *The fact that children are curious in no way reflects on your parenting ability. Nor does it diminish their love for you.* If your child seeks information about his birth parents, you may be afraid you will be cut out of his life, that your family will be disrupted, that he will leave or that he will love you less somehow. You may fear you have been mere baby-sitters. Adoptive parents' greatest fear is that after years of loving and nurturing a child, he will leave them one day for his birth parents.

If you take the position that, by hiding information or obstructing his search, you are protecting your child from harm and hurt, look to yourself. Your ambition may be to *own* him. Impossible, of course, just as it is with any child. You are your child's *real* parents. How could it be otherwise, no matter what he knows or where he goes or whom he meets?

If you are threatened by your child's curiosity, his natural interest in his roots, seek counseling. You must be secure enough to help your child work through the loss issue. The more confident you are as adoptive parents, the stronger base your child will rest on.

When problems occur, keep in mind that adoptive parents are susceptible to overreaction and to self-blame.

"Have I overdisciplined or overindulged?"

"Have I somehow caused my child to feel insecure?"

Do not attribute every behavior problem to adoption. But if your child's behavior is offensive or excessively reclusive, then seek help.

Usually, the identity crisis emerges full-blown at the same time as that of all other children—around adolescence. Be prepared. Realize that it is a matter of identity and not genetics. It will be tempting for you and your child to blame any conflict on adoption, thinking you might understand each other better if you were related by blood. Your teen might fantasize that his birth parents would be more sympathetic to him. He might use adoption as a weapon: "You don't love me enough."

Adoption professionals now place increasing emphasis on post-adoption counseling, focusing on the special issues that confront adoptees throughout life. Many adoption agencies are developing post-adoption services. Take advantage of them.

CHAPTER TEN

The Changing Face of Adoption: Forecast for the '90s

You may be amazed by how many people around you have been directly affected by adoption. When you realize there are an estimated thirty million people in the United States involved with adoption, it is no wonder. Those numbers will continue to grow—and the adoption field will continue to change. Here's what we see happening in the next decade.

• *Adoption will gain in public acceptance as a means of creating a family.*

• *There will continue to be an imbalance in supply and demand of readily available healthy American newborns, although new approaches may help.* Substantial emphasis will be placed on exposing pregnant women to the adoption option.

• *The trend to limit abortion will create a new source of newborn infants available for adoption.*

Increasingly active anti-abortion groups may succeed, on a state-by-state basis, in their efforts to restrict abortion. As a result, more pregnancies may be carried to term and some of the parents involved will consider adoption as their solution to the unexpected birth of a child.

• *Minority adoptions will increase.*

• *Adoption will be increasingly affected by new options open to those wanting to parent.*

Advances in reproductive technology and infertility treatments probably will siphon off some parents from the demand side. Surrogacy may be a possibility for some, although it is entirely possible the practice will be outlawed.

William Pierce of the National Committee for Adoption warns against legitimizing surrogate arrangements: "It is a very short step, legally, from saying that it is acceptable for a woman to accept money for the transfer of a child who is purposefully conceived to saying that a woman may accept money for a child that is accidentally conceived. . . . The practice should be outlawed and . . . adoption agencies should have nothing to do with it."

It is already possible for a child to have any combination of up to five parents: an egg donor, a sperm donor, a woman who provides a womb for the gestation, and the couple who rear the child.

According to Sanford Katz of Boston, a professor and family-law specialist, this poses "a whole mess of legitimacy and adoption questions. . . . All of the adoption statutes in the United States will have to be rewritten."

• *Congenital diseases such as AIDS will affect the field of adoption as the number of infected babies increases.*

Adoptive parents will become more wary of acquired immune deficiency syndrome and severely drug-impaired children, and a whole new class of special-needs children will emerge.

Medical tests to confirm that children are AIDS-free will become more common. Also, the AIDS scare may result in fewer unplanned pregnancies with unknown sexual partners.

• *The trend to private adoptions will continue, because of its success and despite the pressure to the contrary.*

Some states have prohibited or limited the practice of allowing lawyers to place children without going through a state adoption agency. At the same time, the National Committee for Adoption, representing more than 130 non-profit agencies, is seeking a total ban on independent adoptions. Their concerns relate to lack of total services for both adoptive and birth parents, a tendency to overcharge, and inappropriate pressure on birth mothers to give up their babies.

• *Adoptions will not become easier.*

It will become more expensive to identify, gain access to, and care for birth mothers, and adoptive parents who are not able to afford the cost will continue to seek out new ways to adopt. As a result, state-operated foster-adopt programs, foreign adoptions, and special-needs adoption programs will continue to grow.

• *The field will become increasingly litigious.*

As adoption evolves, lawyers will confront a thicket of legal issues ranging from the parental rights of unwed fathers and easing of barriers to transreligious and transracial adoption.

Also, as the stakes increase and as lawyers and others representing adoptive parents gain experience, they will learn how to manipulate the law in their client's favor.

• *The potential for abuse will increase.*

Baby selling probably never will be totally controlled because few parties are willing to prosecute.

• *Birth parents will have more options and be more involved in adoption planning.*

In the past, birth parents were kept from making decisions. They were told, "You give us your baby, we'll place him, and that's all you need to know."

Now birth parents have choices among different types of agencies, offering differing services and varied roles in the selection of the adoptive parents. The particularly well-educated birth parent will begin to understand the relative benefits of placing her baby for adoption in one state as opposed to another.

• *The trend to more openness in all aspects of adoption will continue.*

As birth parents realize their power, they will increasingly insist on having a say in selecting adoptive parents. They want to have control over the destiny of their baby.

One birth mother sums it up. "I think that people want to know what happens to their child. When you turn your child over to an agency, it is like dropping a stone in a lake."

• *As awareness and pressures escalate, more children will be released from the foster-care system and become available for adoption, increasing the number of special-needs adoptees.*

• *More birth fathers will become involved in the adoption process.*

Today, the largest percentage of birth-parent contacts are women. As a result, 50 percent of a child's social history is typically denied to the adoptive parent. That is beginning to change. As birth fathers begin to be recognized and their rightful role as parents acknowledged and validated, their legal rights will be further defined and expanded.

• *Traditional sources of locating adoptable children will continue to shrink.*

As a result, advertising, outreach, and other direct proactive means of birth mother recruitment will become more prevalent. Foreign children will become easier to adopt.

• *Agencies will recognize the need for more post-adoption services.*

One adoption specialist says, "Social workers are not trained to deal with adoptive and birth parents who come back to the agencies for help."

Again, pushed by the increase in special-needs adoptions (for which post-adoptive services are most necessary), more programs are being developed.

• *The numbers of foreign adoptions from developing countries will continue to increase.*

More agencies and organizations will focus on these adoptions, and procedures will be streamlined. Abuses will continue to flourish, especially among those who adopt directly overseas without an experienced intermediary.

• *Adopted children's rights will escalate.*

Their right to search for their birth parents will be validated and they will have increased access to their adoption records.

At the same time, birth parents will be able to search more successfully for their children. The courts will no longer be able to guarantee closed adoptions.

Quite possibly, today's laws, which typically close and seal all adoption records, will be changed. Some states may even allow the retroactive opening of previously closed records.

• *As the field of adoption expands, there will be pressure on the U.S. government to play a role in tabulating statistics.*

In addition, the government may begin setting national-policy standards for adoption practices. As abuses surface, Congress may enact regulatory legislation and attempt to standardize other practices as well.

• *Costs will soar.*

Costs for medical, legal, housing, counseling, transportation, and post-adoptive services will skyrocket. As public officials realize that the cost of adoptions is less than the cost of welfare, some states will begin to subsidize them. States will begin to understand that adoption is a preventive, positive alternative to lifelong dependency on the system.

The bottom line is that adoption is an issue of the future. Looking into the '90s and beyond, one thing is clear: Adoption works, and it will continue to work. It is a fine way to have a family.

Sample Home Study

Realize this is a *sample* home study. There are as many versions as there are home studies. We include this to give you an understanding of the topics covered and the way the information you share may be recorded by the social worker who completes your home study.

Note that, although you have given a great deal of often detailed information, the final home study report is usually quite general, relatively brief, and typically favorable.

DATES OF CONTACT

Mr. and Mrs. Doe attended orientation in June 1989. They were seen individually at the office on July 6,

1989, and jointly at their home on July 15 and August 4, 1989. They attended our adoptive parent workshops on July 20 and August 14, 1989. They also attended a seminar on housing a birth mother on July 10, 1989.

MOTIVATION

This couple has been trying to have children for more than five years. After experiencing an ectopic pregnancy in 1984, Mrs. Doe discovered that she suffers from endometriosis. Mr. and Mrs. Doe have endured a multitude of treatment procedures over the years, including both major and minor surgery. In 1988, Mrs. Doe had a second ectopic pregnancy that resulted in yet more major surgery.

After this pregnancy, they realized that parenting a child is the most important thing to them and decided to begin adoption procedures.

When he first considered adoption, John was able to verbalize his concern about whether he would love an adopted child in the same way as a biological child. He has spent much time talking to other adoptive families and has attended several adoption-support group meetings. He now is sure that he would love any child entrusted to him, and he is very excited about the upcoming adoption.

Jane wants to adopt a child because she is from a large family and cannot imagine a life without children.

She is close to her nieces and nephews and loves celebrating important occasions with them. She is very excited about doing these things with her own children and is thrilled that adoption is an option for her.

Both applicants want to adopt a child because they have always planned to have children and look forward to sharing their lives and experiences with a child.

FEES

The petitioners have paid a fee of $15,000 to their adoption agency. This charge covers home study, placement, postplacement supervision, and finalization costs.

RECORDS CHECK

The applicants were fingerprinted in 1989, and they have no criminal history.

BACKGROUND—MAN

John Doe was born on March 27, 1952, in St. Paul, Minnesota (verified). He is the second of two children born to Andrew and Molly Doe. He is five feet eleven inches tall, weighs 190 pounds, and has brown hair and hazel eyes.

John recalls having a very stable, secure childhood. He was raised in a residential area of St. Paul and lived in the same house until he moved away to college. His father was employed as a manager with a local insurance company and his mother was a homemaker. Although he is close to both of his parents, he was closer to his mother growing up, as she was at home full-time.

John describes his mother as warm and nurturing with a strong value system that she instilled in the children. His father spent time with the children by coaching Little League and being active in school events. Although a loving person, John's father did not express his emotions easily. John hopes that he can be more expressive with his own children. His parents had a good marriage and he recalls them fighting rarely. John and his brother were taught that education was important and that hard work was necessary to achieve goals in life. They had chores to do in the house and learned throughout their upbringing to be responsible for their actions. When John misbehaved as a child, his parents generally disciplined him by removing privileges and talking to him about his behavior.

Extended family was important in John's upbringing, and he hopes that this will be true for his children. His paternal grandparents lived nearby when he was growing up and he saw them frequently. He also had aunts, uncles, and cousins who lived nearby. John's older brother, Daniel, lives in Arizona now with his wife and two children. The families see each other frequently and consider each other close friends. John and Jane love having their niece and nephew spend the night. They are able to visit with the rest of the family in St. Paul at least twice a year and speak with them on the telephone weekly.

The Does' neighborhood in St. Paul was a quiet, residential one, filled with children. John recalls having many friends to play with and could always find a softball or kickball game to join. In addition to being involved in sports, John was also active in the Cub Scouts and Boy Scouts. When he was in high school, John worked after school and during summers to earn spending money and save for college.

After graduating from high school with top honors, John decided to follow in his brother's footsteps and attend the University of Arizona. The warm weather—as well as being close to his brother—appealed to him. He graduated with a B.A. in psychology and worked for a year before deciding to enter law school in 1976. After graduating from law school in 1979, Mr. Doe worked for a local law firm for four years. From this solid base of knowledge, John decided that his greatest interest was in corporate law. He now works for the Founding Games Company in Phoenix with five other lawyers in a fifteen-hundred-person company. Mr. Doe enjoys his work a great deal and is also able to spend leisure time with his family, something that will be increasingly important when a child comes home.

Aside from spending time with his friends and family, John enjoys taking walks with his wheaten terrier, playing golf, and attending sporting events.

His parents, Andrew and Molly Doe, reside at 54 Willow Pond Road, St. Paul, Minnesota. His brother, Daniel Doe, resides at 197 Buxton Road, Mesa, Arizona.

With the exception of his grandparents, John's family is extremely supportive of John and Jane's adoption plan. Once the child is home, John believes his grandparents will welcome the child into their family.

BACKGROUND—WOMAN

Jane Doe was born on June 30, 1953, in Taos, New Mexico (verified). She is the second of five children born to Christine and Warren Elk. She is five feet five inches tall, weighs 120 pounds, and has blond hair and hazel eyes.

Jane grew up in Taos and lived there until she left to attend college. Two of her siblings and her parents still live there. Jane's father and mother have always been very active in the art community in New Mexico. Her father owns a very successful gallery in Taos, and Jane's mother is both a sculptor and a teacher at a local community college. Jane has always felt closer to her father than to her mother, since she and her father have similar personalities.

Because her parents had flexible work hours, either her father or her mother was at home with the children most of the time. Jane hopes that she and John can share parenting roles as much as possible so that their children can also have the benefit of two active and participating parents. Since Jane is the oldest girl, she was expected to assume a fair amount of responsibility for her younger siblings when they were growing up. Jane said that the only time this posed a problem was when she wanted to go out with her friends and had to take one or more of them with her. Jane enjoyed a happy, busy childhood. Although she had to take care of her siblings, she also had ample time to "be a kid." Jane and her siblings were all encouraged to be independent thinkers and to assume some reponsibilities at an early age. Jane feels that a great deal of respect developed among all the family members because their thoughts and actions were valued.

Jane's family gets together at least once a year on a major holiday, and she sees her parents several times a year. Her older brother and one sister live in Taos and also are active in the art community. Another sister lives in California and works in marketing, and her youngest sister lives in Colorado, where she has been a ski instructor for the past two years. Although Jane is close to all of them, she feels that she is closest to her sister in California, and they talk and visit as often as possible.

Jane's maternal grandparents both died when she was young and her father's parents lived on the East

Coast. Therefore, extended family was not overly important in her life. Jane believes that may be why her parents had a large family—to create their own sense of "extended" family.

Jane always loved school and excelled academically. She translated her artistic background into an interest in graphics. Jane did the layout for the high-school yearbook and helped do all the scenery for the senior play. She had a wide circle of friends, many of whom she continues to see regularly. Jane attended the University of Arizona and earned her degree in fine arts in 1975. During college, she was active on the college paper and worked part-time at a graphic-design company. Upon graduation, she became a full-time employee of the company. After five years, she switched companies to attain a supervisory position. Jane enjoys her work and the people whom she interacts with a great deal. However, after all the years of trying to have a family, she is looking forward to taking time off to care for a baby full-time.

In her leisure time, Jane enjoys reading, going to museums, working on projects in her home, and spending time with family and friends.

Her parents, Christine and Warren Elk, live at 58 Delmar Way, Taos, New Mexico. The names and addresses of her siblings are: Jonathan Elk, 6921 Landing Street, Taos, New Mexico; Diana Woods, 28 Cross Road, Taos, New Mexico; Heather Kat, 1930 Seaside Park, San Diego, California; and Justine Elk, 238 Valley Road, Aspen, Colorado.

Jane's entire family is aware of John and Jane's adoption plan. They are all extremely supportive and are looking forward to meeting the new member of the family.

PREVIOUS MARRIAGE—MAN

N/A

PREVIOUS MARRIAGE—WOMAN

N/A

MARRIAGE OF APPLICANTS

The applicants were married on June 14, 1980, in Taos, New Mexico (verified), in a religious ceremony. John and Jane first met in college in 1973. At the time, however, they were both dating other people and were only acquaintances. In 1979, they met again at a party and they began dating after that. They immediately felt that they had a great deal in common and were married sixteen months after they began dating. John was first attracted to Jane because of her independence, compassion, and sense of family. Jane was first attracted to John because she felt that she could "be herself" around him. She likes the nurturing side of him and appreciated the fact that he had firm career goals.

Jane and John rarely fight. When they do disagree, they work it out by discussing the issue until a compromise has been reached. They have a happy, loving marriage and consider themselves best friends.

Working through their infertility was the first crisis they had to deal with as a couple. Although it often was a very difficult experience, they were extremely supportive of each other and drew closer as a couple because of it. The hardest decision was determining when to end medical intervention. They chose to join a support group run by the local Resolve chapter and that proved extremely helpful to them.

CHILDREN OF APPLICANTS

N/A

OTHERS IN THE HOME

N/A

HOME AND NEIGHBORHOOD

The applicants purchased their 2,100-square-foot home in 1985 for $110,000. Their home, currently worth $150,000, is built on three-quarters of an acre and includes four bedrooms, two bathrooms, a kitchen, a living room, a family room, a laundry room, and a two-car garage.

They have three smoke alarms in their home and a fire extinguisher in the kitchen.

The applicants have a swimming pool that is fenced in.

They live in a lovely, middle-class neighborhood that is quiet and residential. It is a comfortable, friendly area with many children of all ages. Their next-door neighbors have become close friends and the two couples frequently spend informal evenings together. Jane and John have a three-year-old, soft-coated wheaten terrier who is the love of their lives. She is a friendly, well-trained dog. The Does plan to introduce her to the new baby but will exercise a great deal of caution and never leave the dog alone with the baby.

FINANCIAL

As verified by the applicants' 1988 income-tax return, their gross income for last year was $72,000.

Their net monthly income combined is $4,888.88. Monthly payments include a house payment of $740, $150 for food, $180 for utilities, $50 for telephone, $60 for gasoline, car payments of $300, and $300 miscellaneous expenses. The applicants have about $3000 left in spendable income, much of which goes into various savings and retirement plans.

Their assets include:

Savings accounts	$ 10,000
Real estate	90,000
Vehicles	22,000
Personal property	85,000
Total assets	$207,000

MEDICAL

In a physician's report dated April 28, 1989, Dr. Janice Bird, located at 2345 Scottsdale Road, Scottsdale, Arizona, states that Mr. Doe's general physical and emotional health is excellent. Dr. Bird feels that Mr. Doe would make an excellent adoptive parent.

In a physician's report dated June 3, 1989, Dr. Bird states that Mrs. Doe's general physical and emotional health is excellent. She has been unable to have a biological child and Dr. Bird feels, without reservation, that Mrs. Doe would make an excellent adoptive mother.

Neither applicant has received any counseling for drug or alcohol abuse or any psychiatric counseling.

RELIGIOUS BACKGROUND

Jane and John are not involved in any organized religion at the present time. They would ensure that their child would be exposed to many different beliefs and attitudes. They feel that all children should be raised with a strong sense of ethics and values.

CHILD DESIRED

Mr. and Mrs. Dow would like a healthy newborn baby without any significant medical problems. They are willing to accept twins and would take a Hispanic child. They would consider a child with some history of alcohol or drug abuse excluding any addictions.

The Indian Child Welfare Act was explained.

ATTITUDES TOWARD CHILDREN

Jane and John hope to instill in their child many of the values that their parents taught them. They want to teach their child to be honest and independent, and to value education. They will teach their child that every person is an individual and should be treated with respect. They also hope that their child will share their closeness with their families.

Both Jane and John believe in showing affection to children with lots of hugs and kisses. In terms of discipline, they believe in consistency and setting limits with children. When it is necessary, they will withdraw privileges. They believe that children should be able to enjoy their youth and not have to grow up too fast. They look forward to family outings, enjoying the outdoors, and special times like birthdays, Christmas, and Halloween. They are aware that a child will limit their spontaneity, but they are looking forward to this limitation in their lives.

LONG-RANGE PLANS FOR THE CHILD

Mr. and Mrs. Doe hope their child wants to attend college. High school would be the minimum amount of schooling expected of the child. They want their child to be happy, and only hope that he or she will be a productive, independent member of society.

The applicants do not have a formal will. They plan to have a will drawn up in the near future. In the event of their deaths, Jane's sister Heather Kat and her husband would be named guardians for their child. In the event of John's death or disability, Jane would work part-time and use a day-care facility for child care. In the event of Jane's death or disability, John would continue to work full-time and hire someone for child care.

FUTURE CONTACT WITH NATURAL PARENTS

Mr. and Mrs. Doe would be very open to having a face-to-face meeting with the birth mother and/or birth father. They are willing to send letters, pictures, and poems through their adoption agency to the birth parents.

The applicants support a search for the natural parents when the child is of age. They also would be open to the natural parents' initiating contact with the child after the age of eighteen.

REFERENCES

The names and addresses of the references are: Christine and Warren Elk, 58 Delmar Way, Taos, New Mexico; Heather and Paul Kat, 1930 Seaside Park, San Diego, California; Andrew and Molly Doe, 54 Willow Pond Road, St. Paul, Minnesota; Dave and Lee Fairlee,

551 East Glen Way, Phoenix, Arizona; and Debbie and Jim Ely, 78 Crown Street, Phoenix, Arizona.

All references felt comfortable leaving a child of their own with the applicants. The references feel that the applicants would make excellent parents.

Christine and Warren Elk are Jane's parents. They have known the applicants as a couple for nine years. They state that John and Jane are a happy, loving couple who would provide an adopted child with a warm and loving home.

Heather and Paul Kat are Jane's sister and brother-in-law. They have known the applicants as a couple for nine years. They state that they have named John and Jane as the guardians for their children in their will and that Jane and John are happily married, loving, bright people who will be excellent parents.

Andrew and Molly Doe are John's parents. They have known the applicants as a couple for nine years. They state that Jane and John will make excellent parents to any biological or adopted child. They believe that any child they adopt will be very fortunate to have them as parents.

Dave and Lee Fairlee are Jane and John's neighbors. They have known them for four years and state that John and Jane are a secure, happy, warm couple who will make wonderful parents. They see them frequently and remark on how comfortable they are as a couple and how helpful to their friends and family they are as well.

Debbie and Jim Ely are college friends of both John

and Jane. They have known them closely as a couple for ten years. They have known them through happy and difficult times and state that, through everything, John and Jane have been loving and supportive to each other. They believe that they will be excellent parents to any child.

EVALUATION

From my observations and all information pertaining to the applicants, I believe the applicants are morally, emotionally, physically, and financially fit to adopt a child.

In working with Jane and John Doe, I find them to be a warm, happy, mature couple. They have a positive attitude toward adoption and I believe they will create a wonderful, secure, loving environment for a child.

RECOMMENDATIONS

It is respectfully recommended that the applicants be certified as acceptable to adopt children in the State of Arizona.

Respectfully submitted,

Susan Antelope
Director of Social Services

Understanding Fees in an Adoption

It can be difficult to explain the large variance in adoption agency costs and fees to a potential adoptive parent. Fees may be $5,000 or less in a state-funded program or in an agency that is subsidized by charitable contributions and considers adoptions "missionary work." At the same time, fees may be as high as $30,000 in a full-service agency in which comprehensive services are offered and adoptive parent fees pay 100 percent of the cost of the program. To help determine whether an agency fee is fair, ask the following questions:

1. What percentage of the adoption program is financed by adoptive parent fees? Is a percentage

of the cost subsidized by other means such as charitable contributions, trusts, endowments, volunteer services, or other free services?

2. What services are provided by the agency and how extensive are these services?
3. Of birth parents who receive adoption agency services, how many place their babies for adoption?

1. WHAT PERCENTAGE OF THE ADOPTION PROGRAM IS FINANCED BY ADOPTIVE PARENT FEES? IS A PERCENTAGE OF THE COST SUBSIDIZED BY OTHER MEANS SUCH AS CHARITABLE CONTRIBUTIONS, TRUSTS, ENDOWMENTS, VOLUNTEER SERVICES, OR OTHER FREE SERVICES?

For the past fifty years, most traditional adoption agencies have operated much like religious organizations, relying on one or more of the following: charitable contributions, trusts, endowments, volunteer work, and donated services. Therefore, these agencies can often charge artificially low fees to adoptive parents.

On the other hand, other adoption agencies operate without the benefit of any type of additional funding or donated services—adoptive parent fees pay all the costs of these programs. The fees charged by agencies of this kind can be high, especially if a full menu of adoption services is provided.

2. WHAT SERVICES ARE PROVIDED BY THE AGENCY AND HOW EXTENSIVE ARE THESE SERVICES?

Many traditional adoption agencies have shifted their focus from adoptions of newborn infants. The term *social service agency* has evolved to describe these organizations, which offer additional services such as foster care, family planning, alcohol- or drug-abuse counseling, and other rehabilitation programs. The commingling of many services can affect budgeting and the quality of services along with personnel.

For instance, an adoption program may have a single social worker who is responsible for providing all services to a client, even though the social worker may not be qualified to give legal advice, make medical arrangements, or deal with adoptive parent insurance. The cost of the adoption program may not be separated from the costs for all the other social services offered by the agency. Often, there is no breakout of the adoption budget, and adoption fees have little relationship to the cost of the work performed in the adoption.

Following is a list of the types of services that may be offered by a full-service adoption agency. Unfortunately, pricing these services is impossible. Legal fees charged by an adoption specialist in New York City might average $200 an hour, whereas the same legal services in South Dakota might run $40 an hour. Depending on where you live, the cost of the doctor and hospital in a normal delivery may range from $1,000 to $7,000. If cost is critical, make an analysis of the kinds of services you need and the cost of the services provided by an agency you are considering, and be certain you know exactly what is and is not included in those costs.

Adoptive Parent Services

- Application.
- Orientation to the agency.
- Home study.
- Supervisory study, postplacement study.
- Adoption education.
- Adoption counseling.
- Pre-adoption support groups.
- Preparation of interstate compact materials if a child is adopted across state lines.
- Post-adoption support groups.
- Post-adoption exchanges of pictures, information, letters, and gifts.
- Adoptive parent insurance review.
- Legal work involving consents, guardianship, termination of parental rights hearings, adoption hearings, and the drafting of all documents necessary for hearings.

Birth Parent Services

- Birth parent housing for one to nine months.
- Maternity clothing.
- Food and personal care packages.
- Prenatal medical care.
- Doctor and hospital charges including C-section delivery, and any other additional medical expenses.
- Counseling for the biological mother and father.
- Legal services for the biological mother and father.
- Transportation to agency appointments and/or medical appointments.
- Pre-adoption birth parent support groups where birth parents discuss issues such as employment, education, parenting, and, of course, adoption and its impact on them.
- Preparation of medical and social history of the biological family.
- Parenting classes for those birth parents who decide against adoption.
- Post-adoption support groups including post-adoption grief counseling.
- Post-adoption exchanges of pictures, information, letters, and gifts.

Additional Agency Expenses That May Be Paid For by Adoptive Parents

- Rent.
- Insurance.
- Staffing.
- Phone.
- Mailing.
- Xeroxing of files.
- Baby pickup from hospital.
- Foster care of babies.
- Advertising.
- Accounting.
- Maintenance of manuals and compliance with other policies and procedures mandated by state licensing regulations.
- Lobbying for effective adoption laws, policies, and procedures.
- Public relations including outreach to the community.

Although this list is not complete, it does help you compare costs.

3. OF BIRTH PARENTS WHO RECEIVE ADOPTION AGENCY SERVICES, HOW MANY PLACE THEIR BABIES FOR ADOPTION?

The actual number of placements affects adoption costs too. Many adoption agencies factor the cost of failed adoptions into their fees. Consider the fiscal 1989 statistics of the Southwest Adoption Center, Inc.: services were provided to 351 birth parents, although only 100 actually placed a child for adoption. Adoptive parents provided 100 percent of the funding for the adoption program with the understanding that the fees they paid provided services to many birth parents who would decide to keep their children rather than place them for adoption. The free services provided to birth parents substantially escalate the overall costs to adoptive parents.

4. A SPECIAL NOTE: ADOPTING ACROSS STATE LINES

If you are adopting across state lines, understand that compact administrators rarely give immediate approval to take your child home. Thus, assuming you must wait, the critical issue is: How will your child be cared for until he is in your custody? Many states will not allow you to care for your child while waiting for compact approval because you are not an approved foster care family for that state. You may not even be allowed to visit, because foster care providers are often underpaid and not set up to facilitate supervised home visitation. Plus, to avoid emotional trauma in the event the adoption is denied, some adoption professionals do not want you to see or bond with the child before you are legally approved to take him home.

If you are not working through a licensed adoption agency which provides foster care as part of your agreement, this process may add several thousand dollars to your adoption costs. In cases where foster care cannot be found, newborn infants will have to wait in the hospital at several hundred dollars per day. Be particularly wary of inexperienced attorneys who have few, if any, dealings with interstate placements. Even clerical errors can cause further delay. When doing interstate placements it's best to use an adoption agency. Almost always they are licensed for foster home care, and you will have the reassurance of knowing that your child is receiving proper care. But remember, depending on your state's policy, your child may be two weeks old before you first see him.

Information Guide

This list encompasses various resources from varying perspectives for a wide variety of people—adoptive parents, children, friends, and so on. It is not all-inclusive, but it will serve as a springboard for you to begin gathering information about adoption and related issues. The resources listed, in turn, will provide more information about state agencies, organizations, and so on that will advance you yet another step forward.

SELECTED BOOKS, BROCHURES, AND DIRECTORIES

General

Gilman, Lois. *The Adoption Resource Book.* Harper & Row, Publishers, New York, 1984.
This comprehensive guide to adoption is aimed at potential adoptive parents. Includes positive descriptions of independent as well as agency adoption. Also included is a brief account of open adoption and the advantages associated with openness. A state-by-state domestic adoption directory lists nearly a thousand agencies along with names and addresses of parent groups, exchanges, public service offices, and other sources.

Johnston, Patricia Irwin. *An Adoptor's Advocate.* Perspectives Press, Fort Wayne, Indiana, 1984.
Focuses on the issues facing adoptive couples as they plan family building through adoption. Author mentions open adoption briefly and provides a good discussion of society's feelings about adoption.

Johnston, Patricia Irwin. *Perspectives on a Grafted Tree.* Perspectives Press, Fort Wayne, Indiana, 1983.
A beautiful collection of poems written by birth parents, adoptees, adoptive parents, and extended family members. They express a wide variety of the feelings of gain and loss, happiness and pain, felt by all those touched by adoption.

Lifton, Betty Jean. *Lost and Found.* The Dial Press, New York, 1979.
A powerful, eloquent journey through the emotional labyrinth of the adoption experience. The book uses personal case histories to examine adoption from all perspectives. For example: What is it like to be adopted? What are the inner forces that compel some people to search for their birth parents? What happens after the reunion?

Lindsay, Jeanne Warren. *Open Adoption: A Caring Option.* Morning Glory Press, Buena Park, California, 1987.
Explores the differing degrees of openness available through agencies in various parts of the United States. Gives some historical perspective on the move toward open adoption and examines trends by discussing specific cases. Written by an educator who believes the move toward openness is making adoption more acceptable to young pregnant women.

Melina, Lois Ruskai. *Raising Adopted Children.* Harper & Row, Publishers, New York, 1986.
A complete book for adoptive parents and professionals that reassures adoptive parents and offers advice and basic information on issues ranging from bonding and attachment to adolescence and adulthood.

Rillera, Mary Jo, and Sharon Kaplan. *Cooperative Adoption: A Handbook.* Triadoption Library, Inc., Westminster, California, 1984.
Guidelines for birth parents and adoptive parents planning an open adoption. Authors do not recommend co-parenting except in the sense that both sets of parents should be actively involved with the child. The adoptive parents are the legal and psychological day-to-day parents, but the birth parents may be as close to the adoptive family as desired by everyone involved. Suggested cooperative adoption documents are included.

Schaffer, Patricia. *How Babies and Families Are Made.* Tabor Sarah Books, Berkeley, California, 1988.
A fascinating approach to the concept of "family" and how families are made.

Silber, Kathleen, and Phylis Speelin. *Dear Birth Mother, Thank You for Our Baby.* Corona Publishing Company, San Antonio, 1983.
A beautiful description of the advantages of open adoption. Rebuts what the authors call the four myths of adoption: (1) "the birth

mother obviously doesn't care about her child or she wouldn't have given him away"; (2) "secrecy in every phase of the adoption process is necessary to protect all parties"; (3) "both the birth mother and birth father will forget about their unwanted child"; (4) "if the adoptee really loved his adoptive family, he would not have to search for his birth parents."

Sorosky, Arthur, Annette Baran, and Reuben Pannor. *The Adoption Triangle: The Effects of the Sealed Record on Adoptees, Birth Parents, and Adoptive Parents.* Anchor Press/Doubleday, Garden City, New York, 1978.
The authors evaluate adoption policies. Contains interviews and correspondence with hundreds of adoptees, birth parents, and adoptive parents, plus profiles the central problems and issues. Urges reform.

Children and Teens

Brodzinsky, Anne Braff. *The Mulberry Bird.* Perspectives Press, Fort Wayne, Indiana, 1986.
Uses one mother and her baby bird to illustrate why a birth parent would place her child for adoption. Tells the adoption story in a positive way that enhances a child's self-esteem. It is also an educational tool for *non*-adopted children. For ages 5–12.

Jewett, Claudia L. *Helping Children Cope with Separation and Loss.* The Harvard Common Press, Harvard, Massachusetts, 1982.
Helps parents and professionals deal with children who have had major losses in their lives. A practical plan for helping children through the recovery process. Helps to distinguish behavior that may immediately follow a loss from the long-lasting behavior that may appear in a child who suffered a loss years ago and never resolved it.

Koch, Janice. *Our Baby: A Birth and Adoption Story.* Perspectives Press, Fort Wayne, Indiana, 1985.

For adopted children integrating information about conception and human sexuality into the adoption story, underlining the fact that an adoptee has the same beginnings as any other person. This book mentions the idea of birth parents but not in detail, as it is for children ages 2–7. Contends that the adoption homecoming is a positive experience for the family.

Krementz, Jill. *How It Feels to Be Adopted.* Alfred A. Knopf, New York, 1982.
Interviews and photographs detail the stories of nineteen different adopted children ages 9–16. Excellent for adults who want to understand the often unspoken thoughts of adopted children and for children in those age groups. Not appropriate for preschool children.

Lifton, Betty Jean. *I'm Still Me.* Alfred A. Knopf, New York, 1981.
A novel for adoptees of junior- and senior-high-school age, about an adopted high-school girl who confronts her own roots when assigned to draw a family tree.

Nerlove, Evelyn. *Who Is David?* Child Welfare League of America, Inc., Washington, D.C., 1985.
Story of an adopted adolescent and how he deals with his fears and questions about adoption. It is great reading for adoptive parents, professionals, and adolescents.

Schlein, Miriam. *The Way Mothers Are.* Albert Whitman and Company, Niles, Illinois, 1963.
A delightful book about attachment/bonding and unconditional love. It is a good story to read to preschoolers and younger children, both adopted and non-adopted.

Sly, Kathleen O'Conner. *Becky's Special Family.* Alternative Parenting Publications, Corona, California, 1985.
A straightforward picture book for children about open adoption

written from the perspective of the child. There are blank pages at the end where adopted children can put pictures of both their adoptive and birth families, since "both of my families are very special."

Stein, Sara Bonnett. *The Adopted One.* Walker & Company, New York, 1986.
This book for toddlers and young children has wonderful photographs that can stand alone even without the very good text, so that parent and child can develop their own stories. The double text—one set for children and another set for adults that serves as a resource for handling children's questions and comments about adoption—deals with "feelings" of adoption in an open and healthy way.

ADOPTION SUPPORT

Holmes, Pat. *Supporting an Adoption.* Our Child Press, Wayne, Pennsylvania, 1986.
Intended for the family and friends of an adoptive or pre-adoptive family. Explains how they can be helpful to an adoptive family. Discusses what and what not to say, visiting hours, families' adjustment, and the adoption process.

HISTORY OF ADOPTION

Aigner, Hal. *Adoption in America: Coming of Age.* Paradigm Press, Providence, Rhode Island, 1986.
The history of adoption in the United States.

Kirk, David H. *Adoptive Kinship: A Modern Institution in Need of Reform.* Ben-Simon Publications, Port Angeles, Washington, 1981.
Review of the civil rights of adoptees. Kirk claims that the difficulties peculiar to adoptive family life stem from well-meant but mistaken laws and administrative practices. He suggests new di-

rections for adoption, as a social institution and as it affects human relationships.

Birth Mothers

Arms, Suzanne. *To Love and Let Go.* Alfred A. Knopf, New York, 1983.
The stories of several young women who release their babies for adoption and of the parents these birth mothers choose. Arms's emphasis is on the needs of the birth mothers and on the positive effects when adoptive parents and birth parents meet and develop a relationship.

Lindsay, Jeanne Warren. *Pregnant Too Soon: Adoption Is an Option.* Morning Glory Press, Buena Park, California, 1988.
Young women who were "pregnant too soon" tell their stories. Most released their children for adoption and share their reasons for doing so. Included with the personal stories is information on agency and independent adoption, fathers' rights, dealing with grief, and other aspects of adoption. Written for young birth mothers, but may also give adoptive parents added empathy for these young people.

Infertility

Johnston, Patricia Irwin. *Understanding.* Perspectives Press, Fort Wayne, Indiana, 1985.
For the family and friends of an infertile person or couple. This booklet is *not* about adoption, but it lets people know how they can be supportive of those who are dealing with infertility. Corrects myths about infertility and educates people about the extent of the loss and the grieving process involved.

Mason, Mary Martin. *The Miracle Seekers: An Anthology of Infertility.* Perspectives Press, Fort Wayne, Indiana, 1987.

Twenty short stories exploring feelings and issues relating to infertility with humor, pathos, pain, and determination. The message is: You are not alone.

Menning, Barbara E. *Infertility: A Guide for the Childless Couple.* Prentice-Hall, Inc., Englewood Cliffs, New Jersey, 1977.

Directories of Adoption Agencies in Each State

Plumez, J. H., *Successful Adoption.* Harmony Books, New York, 1982.

Gilman, Lois. *The Adoption Resource Book.* Harper & Row, Publishers, New York, 1984.
Lists private and public agencies in each state.

International Concerns Committee for Children. *Report on Foreign Adoption.* International Concerns Committee for Children, Boulder, Colorado, 1988.
Also lists home study agencies in each state.

National Committee for Adoption. *Adoption Factbook.* National Committee for Adoption, Washington, D.C., 1989.

Directories of State and Regional Adoption Exchanges and Photo-Listing Services

National Committee for Adoption. *Adoption Factbook.* National Committee for Adoption, Washington, D.C., 1989.

Plumez, J. H. *Successful Adoption.* Harmony Books, New York, 1982.

State-by-State Adoption Facts, Regulations, and Statutes

Association of Administrators of the Interstate Compact on the Placement of Children. *Survey of States Party to ICPC (December*

1987). Available from the American Public Welfare Association, 1125 Fifteenth Street N.W., Suite 300, Washington, D.C. 20005.

National Committee for Adoption. *Adoption Factbook.* National Committee for Adoption, Washington, D.C., 1989.

DIRECTORIES OF PARENT ASSOCIATIONS AND SUPPORT GROUPS

Bolles, E. P. *The Penguin Adoption Handbook.* Penguin Books, New York, 1984.

National Committee for Adoption. *Adoption Factbook.* National Committee for Adoption, Washington, D.C., 1989.

ADOPTION COORDINATORS IN CANADA

BRITISH COLUMBIA

Adoption Coordinator
Family and Children's Services
Ministry of Social Services and Housing
Parliament Buildings
Victoria, British Columbia
V8W 3A2
(604) 387-7059

ALBERTA

Program Supervisor
Adoption Services
Department of Social Services

Seventh Street Plaza, 12th Floor
10030 107th Street
Edmonton, Alberta
T5J 3E4
(403) 422-0178

Saskatchewan

Program Manager
Adoption Services
Family Support Division
Department of Social Services
1920 Broad Street, 12th Floor
Regina, Saskatchewan
S4P 3V7
(306) 787-5698

Manitoba

Adoption Coordinator
Adoptions and Field Services
Department of Community Services
114 Garry Street
Winnipeg, Manitoba

Ontario

Adoption Policy and Program Planning
Children's Services Branch
Ministry of Community and Social Services
700 Bay Street, 2nd Floor, Suite 209
Toronto, Ontario
M7A 1E9
(416) 963-0709

Québec

Directeur
Secrétariat à l'adoption internationale
3700 rue Berri
Montréal, Québec
H2L 4G9
(514) 873-5226

New Brunswick

Program Consultant for Adoption Service
Department of Health and Community Services
P.O. Box 5100
Fredericton, New Brunswick
E3B 5G8
(506) 453-3830

Nova Scotia

Coordinator, Children in Care
Family and Children's Services
Department of Social Services
P.O. Box 696
Halifax, Nova Scotia
B3J 2T7
(902) 424-3205

Prince Edward Island

Coordinator, Children in Care
Department of Health and Social Services
P.O. Box 2000
Charlottetown, Prince Edward Island
C1A 7N8
(902) 368-4931; (902) 368-4932

Newfoundland

Assistant Director of Child Welfare Services
Department of Social Services
Confederation Building
3rd Floor, West Block
P.O. Box 4750
St. John's, Newfoundland
A1C 5T7
(709) 576-2667

Northwest Territories

Program Officer, Child Welfare
Family and Children's Services
Department of Social Services
Government of the Northwest Territories
Yellowknife, Northwest Territories
X1A 2L9
(403) 873-7943

Yukon Territory

Placement and Support Services Supervisor
Department of Health and Human Resources
P.O. Box 2703
Whitehorse, Yukon Territory
Y1A 2C6
(403) 667-3002

Glossary

ABANDONMENT: Giving up the responsibility to parent a child, usually by leaving the child's life without ensuring the child's care for the future. Disappearing without making arrangements for child care.

ADOPTEE: A person who has been adopted.

ADOPTION: The legal process by which parental rights are transferred from birth parents to adoptive parents; may include an array of professional and social services to adoption triad members.

ADOPTION AGENCY: Any person or organization placing children in adoptive homes, under the jurisdiction of state or provincial licensing laws.

ADOPTION AGENCY CLIENTS: Birth parents, their families, their children, and prospective and actual adoptive families receiving adoption-related services through an adoption agency.

ADOPTION FACILITATOR: A person or organization that helps coordinate an adoption, typically nonlicensed.

ADOPTION PROFESSIONAL: Employee of a licensed adoption agency or a trained and educated adoption authority who has training and experience in adoption services, and authorization by the agency to provide adoption services.

ADOPTION RECORDS: All records, files, and documents pertaining to an adoption.

ADOPTION SUBSIDY: A grant provided by the state to the adoptive parents of a child with special needs, either as a maintenance subsidy or for special services, or both.

ADOPTION TRIAD OR TRIANGLE: The three integral parties to an adoption—the adoptee, the adoptive parents, and the birth parents.

ADOPTIVE PARENT: Any person who legally assumes parental rights and responsibilities for an adopted child.

ADOPTIVE PARENT APPLICANT: An individual who has applied to be an adoptive parent.

AGENCY: A person or organization, usually licensed by the state, that places children for adoption. Also, a division of state government or a child welfare bureau that is authorized to provide adoption or foster care services.

AGENCY ADOPTION: An adoption coordinated by a state-licensed adoption agency.

AGENCY CHECKLIST: A checklist used to evaluate agencies and other adoption organizations.

AGENCY PLACEMENT: Completion of an adoption.

APPLICATION: Completion of the required adoption application forms for home study, placement, etc.

BIOLOGICAL CHILD: The child of parents by birth.

BIRTH CERTIFICATE: *Original*—The legal document issued at the time of birth with the child's biological history including the identity of one or both biological parents. *Amended*—The legal document after the adoption is finalized, replacing the original birth certificate, as indicated by the court in the adoption decree, with the adoptive family names replacing the birth family names.

BIRTH FAMILY: All biological relatives of an adoptee.

BIRTH PARENTS: Biological parents who conceive and/or give birth to a child and who then surrender their legal rights to the child.

BLACK MARKET: The illegal buying or selling of children.

BONDING: The feeling of caring and love that unites a family.

CHILD: Any person who has not reached the age of majority as defined by state law.

CLOSED ADOPTION: An adoption in which confidentiality of both the adoptive parents and the birth parents is protected under the law and in which all records are sealed by the court.

CLOSED RECORDS: Adoption records that are legally closed by the courts and thus unavailable to anyone looking for adoption information.

CONSENT FORM: The legal document signed by the biological mother and father allowing their child to be placed for adoption. If a birth parent is unavailable, the courts can validate the consents without the birth parent's signature. (A consent is also known as a *surrender* or *relinquishment.*)

CONTACT: Various forms of communication between a prospective adoptive parent and a possible adoptee that help facilitate the adoption process—for example, visits, phone conversations, counseling, and letters.

COOPERATIVE ADOPTION: An adoption in which the adopted child has access to both his adoptive parents and his birth parents and participates in decisions affecting his life.

CUSTODY: Charge exercised by a person or an authority, embodying all of the following rights and responsibilities:

- The right to have physical possession of a child.
- The right and the duty to protect, train, and discipline a child.
- The responsibililty to provide a child with food, shelter, education, and ordinary medical care, and the authority to consent

to surgery or other extraordinary medical care in an emergency.

DEVELOPMENTAL DISABILITY: Any handicapping condition related to delays in maturation of, or difficulty with, skills or intellect.

DIRECT PLACEMENT ADOPTION: An adoption proceeding in which the birth parents sign consents specifically naming the adoptive parents.

DISRUPTION: The dissolution of an adoption, as, for example, in the case of a couple who try to parent a handicapped child only to learn that they lack the tools to cope.

DOCUMENTATION: A collection of written data concerning the child, birth parents, and adoptive parents.

FINAL ADOPTION DECREE: The legal document issued by the court that completes an adoption.

FINALIZATION: Court action that grants permanent legal custody of a child to the adoptive parents.

FOREIGN ADOPTION: Obtaining a child from a foreign country for the purpose of adoption by United States citizens.

FOSTER ADOPTION PLACEMENT: The placement of a child—adoption being the goal—with a couple who are certified as suitable to adopt and whose home is licensed as a foster home. There is no assurance that the placement will evolve into an adoption.

FOSTER CARE: Substitute parental care for a short, extended, or permanent period of time for a child whose own family cannot provide care. Care may be in a private or group facility.

FOSTER CHILD: A child who is placed with a state-licensed family or in a group-care facility because his own family cannot provide care.

FOSTER PARENT: A state-licensed adult who is paid to take care of a child for a short, extended, or permanent period of time but is not related to the child by blood, marriage, or adoption.

FOSTER PARENT ADOPTION: The legal adoption of a child by parents who have served as foster parents for the child prior to the adoption.

HARD-TO-PLACE CHILD: A child for whom it is difficult to find suitable adoptive parents, usually because he is an older child or an emotionally or physically handicapped child.

HIGH RISK OF PHYSICAL OR MENTAL DISORDER: High probability that a child possesses a debilitating physical or mental disorder, as determined by a professional authority and as defined by accepted medical standards.

HOME STUDY: A study of the home of prospective adoptive parents, normally completed prior to placement of a child in that home. A home study validates suitability to adopt. Although rare, a negative evaluation almost always means that the adoption will not be authorized.

IDENTIFIED ADOPTION: A type of adoption that involves the location by potential adoptive parents, or by someone on their behalf, of a birth parent willing to consider adoption. The identity of the adoptive parents and birth parent may or may not be known to each other.

INDEPENDENT ADOPTION: An adoption arranged privately by a nonlicensed third party such as a doctor, lawyer, or adoption facilitator, or between the birth family and adoptive parents. There are three types of independent adoptions:

- *Intermediary Placement*—An adoption arranged by an intermediary, who is most often a doctor or lawyer.
- *Direct Placement*—An adoption arranged between birth parent(s) and adoptive parent(s) known to the birth parent(s).
- *Relative Adoption*—An adoption by someone related to the child by birth or marriage; most commonly, an adoption involving a stepparent who legally adopts a spouse's child.

INFERTILITY: Inability to conceive or carry a pregnancy to term.

INTERLOCUTORY DECREE: An interim decree of adoption (usually finalized at some later date, typically after a satisfactory report to the court of the adopted child's postplacement adjustment).

INTERMEDIARY: A third party who acts as a go-between in any phase of an adoption or search.

INTERNATIONAL ADOPTION: Adoption of a child from a country other than the one in which the child was born.

INTERSTATE COMPACT: The legal compact among states that allows for the placement of children for adoption across state lines.

JUVENILE COURT: Usually, the division of a state's superior court devoted to matters concerning children under the age of majority.

LEGAL-RISK ADOPTION: An adoption proceeding that is started even though the prospective adoptive family cannot be guaranteed that the child is adoptable because of one of the following:

- Continuing desire of the biological parents to parent.
- Pending legal action contesting the validity of a voluntary surrender or the legal authority of a court order involuntarily terminating parental rights.

LICENSE: A legal authorization to operate an adoption agency, issued by a state authority.

MAINTENANCE SUBSIDY: An ongoing monthly payment for the support of an adopted child, usually one with special needs.

MENTAL DISABILITY: A lifelong condition characterized by impaired intellectual development that limits one's ability to function independently, as defined by accepted national standards and diagnosed by a physician or child-development specialist.

MINORITY CHILDREN: Children of partially or completely non-Caucasian parentage. Also, children of mixed Caucasian and non-Caucasian heritage.

NON-IDENTIFYING INFORMATION: The medical and social history and other information exchanged between birth parents and an adoptive family without using the name and address of the parties.

OPEN ADOPTION: Usually, an adoption in which the birth parents and adoptive parents meet. Names and addresses may be exchanged, and communication between the parties may continue beyond the meeting.

OPEN RECORDS: Adoption records open to all members of the adoption triad—the birth family, the adoptive family, and the adoptee.

ORPHAN: A child deprived by death of both biological parents.

PETITION: A written request to a court by an adoptive parent for legal custody, guardianship, and/or adoption of a child.

PHOTO-LISTING: Publication of photographs of children available for adoption.

POST-LEGAL ADOPTION SERVICES: An array of social services delivered to any member of the triad following a legal adoption, such as counseling and adoption support groups.

PREGNANCY COUNSELING: Counseling on the adoption process, pregnancy, or parenting offered to birth parents and their families during a pregnancy.

RELINQUISH: The legal act by which birth parents consent to an adoption and give up all legal rights to a child so that the adoption can take place.

RESCISSION: A period of time in which a person is allowed to revoke a legal document.

REUNION REGISTRY: A passive registry search system through which triad members and significant others in the family may be identified to each other for possible reunion.

SEALED RECORDS: Adoption records legally closed to all members of the adoption triad.

SEARCH: The process undertaken to determine and/or locate an adoptee's birth family.

SOCIAL HISTORY: Information about a person's background, including (but not limited to) the following:

- Upbringing.
- Personality.
- Interests.
- Hobbies.
- Schooling.
- Work.
- Attitudes.

SPECIAL-NEEDS CHILDREN: Children characterized by one or more of the following:

- Physical, mental, or developmental disability, or high risk for any of these.
- Emotional disturbances.
- An age of six years or more at the time of application for adoption.
- Emotional or physical problems created by ethnic or racial factors.
- Disturbances caused by removal from significant relationships (foster care, parents, siblings, etc.).

SPECIAL SERVICES SUBSIDY: Payment for services related to the special needs of an adopted child.

SUCCESSFUL ADOPTION: Adoption in which:

- A child's basic needs (nurture, stimulation, continuity, reciprocity) are met.
- There is a mutual bonding between parent and child, along with a commitment through childhood and a lifelong sense of belonging.
- There is no severe social or physiological dysfunction due to the adoption.

SUPERVISORY STUDY: A study done after a child has been placed in an adoptive parent home, but prior to the final adoption hearing. The study reports whether bonding has taken place, whether the child and/or parents are having any unforeseen difficulties in adjustment, whether the child has any medical problems, and any other important matters concerning the parents and child.

SURRENDER: A legal document signed by birth parent(s) to terminate their parental rights and responsibilities for their child; the act of terminating parental rights and responsibilities, which can be voluntary or court-ordered. Surrender may be referred to as *relinquishment* or *consent,* in some states.

TRIAD: The three categories of persons directly involved in an adoption—adoptee(s), birth parent(s), and adoptive parent(s).

Index